Bike-Ways

The popular 3-speed lightning bike is being replaced by the 10 speed (5 rear sprockets and 2 front chain wheels).

Bike-Ways

(101 Things to Do with a Bike)

New Revised Edition

BY
LILLIAN and
GODFREY FRANKEL

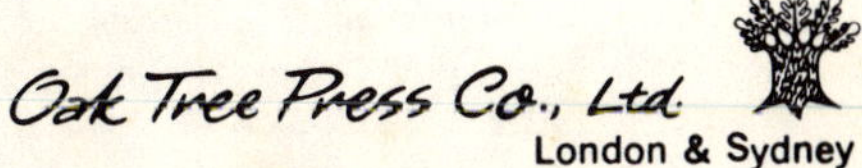

BOOKS BY THE FRANKELS

Creating from Scrap
101 Best Action Games for Boys
101 Best Games for Girls

ACKNOWLEDGMENTS

The authors wish to thank the following organizations for furnishing photographs and resource material: Bicycle Institute of America, Inc., American Youth Hostels, Girl Scouts of America, Boy Scouts of America, *American Bicyclist*, Amateur Bicycle League of America, Bicycle Information Bureau, American Automobile Association, U.S. Rubber Company, Minnesota Mining and Manufacturing Company, Standard Oil Company of New Jersey, National Park Service, Arlington, Virginia, Police Department, National Film Board of Canada, Bob's Cycle Shop, New York City, Columbia Manufacturing Company, Stelber Cycle Corp., and Schwinn Bicycle Company.

Seventh Printing, 1973

Sterling Publishing Co., Inc.
419 Park Avenue South, New York, N.Y. 10016
British edition published by Oak Tree Press Co., Ltd., Nassau, Bahamas
Distributed in Australia and New Zealand by Oak Tree Press Co., Ltd.,
P.O. Box 34, Brickfield Hill, Sydney 2000, N.S.W.
Distributed in the United Kingdom and elsewhere in the British Commonwealth
by Ward Lock Ltd., 116 Baker Street, London W 1

Manufactured in the United States of America
Library of Congress Catalog Card No.: 61-15857
ISBN 0-8069-4004-2 UK 7061 2303 4
4005-0

Contents

Introduction

With the current concern in trying to save the world from various forms of pollution, it is little wonder that the bicycle is now enjoying a renaissance.

The bicycle is the simplest, most economical and most efficient method of transportation invented by man. It takes very little storage space when not in use, can carry as much as ten times its own weight, requires very little maintenance, moves noiselessly without fuel over almost any kind of road or narrow path, and is free from the useless accessories which have become characteristic of modern cars.

In this day and age its simplicity is amazing—two wheels, two pedals, a chain and sprocket, a frame, a seat and handlebars!

There is no better way to know the land and feel a part of it. The sweep of the countryside, the layout of the city, the architectural achievement and even lack of achievement, are there to behold and ponder over in a more intimate sort of way. More senses are involved. The field of vision opens up to 180 degrees without dirty windshields and noxious smelling noisy engines. You are the source of power quietly and confidently.

The uses of the bicycle are almost endless, from purely recreational to a regular means of transportation. For the youngster it is his first transportation vehicle, a way to get around and to have fun. For the adult, it provides an excellent recreational outlet, a splendid form of exercise and increasingly, a way to get to work. Many of our large urban centers are establishing protected bike lanes to encourage cyclists to ride to work and decrease the auto traffic pressure.

And that's what this book is about. Its purpose is to help you obtain more enjoyment and greater use of your bike. This book contains hints on learning to ride a bike, selecting a bike, and caring for a bike. There are detailed ideas on playing bike games, planning tours, camping suggestions and club and community events.

We hope we can help you enjoy your spin down a quiet country road, and the pure thrill of coasting down a steep hill, with the hum of the spokes and the whistling of the wind in your ears.

LILLIAN AND GODFREY FRANKEL

Called a "Run-A-Bout," this novel pint-sized bike needs no tools for fast folding. Another attraction is its convenient portability.

Bike Clubs and Community Activities

HOW TO ORGANIZE A BIKE CLUB

If you are like most people, you enjoy sharing your interests with others. To get the most from cycling, you may want to form a bike club with friends in your neighborhood. Such a club can plan outings, go camping and hosteling, or organize such special events as a bike rodeo. Members can help each other repair their cycles and exchange information about equipment, trips, games and club business.

If your club-sponsored rodeos, races, pageants and other events become regular affairs, they will be worthy of reporting in your community newspaper. You can campaign for bike lanes in city parks and on highways and for the improvement of traffic laws affecting cyclists. Individual cyclists are powerless to sponsor any of these activities, but a group can have great influence in the community.

Another advantage of a club is that you can purchase bicycle parts and equipment very economically on a group plan. Your club may be able to get quantity discounts, resulting in substantial savings to each member. You may even be able to extend group purchasing to such items as cameras, small bike radios and clothing.

But first, how do you go about starting a club? Naturally, you will need a meeting place. Perhaps your club can meet in a community center, a "Y," or in a school or college. Club rooms are often available and a meeting place in an established institution will lend prestige to your group. If you meet in a community center or use the facilities of a Scout troop, there is another advantage: a leader may be assigned to you who will contribute the organizing skill a youth group often needs to find its proper direction.

You may also have access to a mimeograph machine for turning out announcements and publicity. Moreover, an established organization is a good resource for recruiting members, and a channel for reaching out and becoming better known in the community. Your bike club can easily become part of other community center activities.

While you are searching for a meeting place, you should also spend some time recruiting members. Speak to your cycle friends to start the ball rolling. Many cyclists know each other from repeated meetings in the local bike repair shop. Here bike data and lingo are traded, and sometimes give-and-take between customers creates the atmosphere of an actual bike club meeting.

Where else can you find prospective members? Right in your own school and neighborhood. You can put up posters calling for interested cyclists in public buildings, such as social service agencies, "Y"s, schools, the city hall, the post office, and in the shops of bike dealers and repairmen. Newspapers and radio stations will also assist in publicizing your invitation to prospective members.

Most local newspapers carry a column listing club announcements. Get in touch with the sports editor or sports columnist and ask him to print your news items. Knowing these writers will be invaluable later when you plan a bike rodeo or a race meet and want proper news coverage. Local radio stations will often accept spot announcements from nonprofit organizations, especially if the news is of civic interest.

If you are interested in a bike and hostel club, write to American Youth Hostels, Inc. 20 West 17th Street, New York, New York 10011 and get their manual on HOW TO FORM AN AMERICAN YOUTH HOSTEL CLUB.

HOW TO PLAN A BIKE PROGRAM

Once you have enough members to begin, you enter the second phase of club organization: setting a common goal. Everyone is interested in his bike and in cycle activities, but what kinds of activities should your club plan? Six members may only be interested in racing; six others, with no interest in racing, may want to go on outings and tours.

This problem of different aims plagues not only bike clubs, but all organizations. One way to obtain agreement is to have a majority vote, but this is not the best method—someone is bound to be dissatisfied. It is best, of course, to include everyone's interest if you can. When there are differences in interest, the common club goal should include so many activities that the entire group will be pleased.

After some discussion your group may decide to limit its activities to racing and touring at the start, and those members interested in other activities may be willing to postpone their choices till later. The central principle to keep in mind is that each member's tastes should be taken into consideration. Then the club will mean something special to every member. Since the program will determine what the club actually does, this phase of club organization is very important.

At the same time that you are all discussing the club's goal, it is wise to draw up a simple constitution or a set of bylaws, so your organization can govern itself smoothly. You will probably want to elect regular officers. In addition, you can form committees, each representing one phase of the club's activities. Committee members may be elected, appointed or simply asked to volunteer. It often works out well if members volunteer for their favorite committee—those people interested in outings join the outing committee, those looking forward to racing join the racing committee, and so on.

A simple constitution should include: a statement of the purposes and goals decided on; provision for the election of officers (usually president, vice-president, secretary and treasurer); mention of a regular meeting time and schedule of dues; a listing of operating committees to plan program activities (trips, parades, racing and organizing a rodeo), social affairs and the handling of the club's publicity. The constitution alone will not make your club successful, but it will help. The real key to the success of your group will be found in the spirit of the members and in the satisfaction they derive from their club experience.

Travelers newly arrived at an A Y H hostel in Holland check their bikes before getting set for the night.

Now that you have members, some publicity, a common goal, and a constitution, you will want to advance your program of activity. Therefore, you may wish to exchange information with other clubs to find out what they are doing. You can accomplish this by joining some of the national bike organizations and by subscribing to magazines.

There are two well known cycling magazines in this country. The *Bicycling!* (formerly *American Cycling*) subscription office is located at 234 Montgomery St., San Francisco, California, 94104. This magazine is directed to the cycle enthusiast. The price for 10 monthly issues, March through December, is $6.00.

The *American Bicyclist and Motorcyclist's* subscription office is at 461 Eighth Ave., New York, N.Y. 10001. An annual subscription is $4.00 for 12 monthly issues. This magazine is geared mostly to the retail trade. A North American Bicycle Atlas published and sold by the American Youth Hostels is available for $1.95. It contains routes and maps of bicycle tours throughout the United States and Canada.

The most highly organized national bicycle group is American Youth Hostels, Inc., described more fully on pages 42-43. It is a nonprofit agency which includes adults as well as younger members. It strives to cultivate a love for the countryside and a broad understanding of the world and of people. One of its goals is to encourage the use of hostels (overnight shelters), where face-to-face associations with people from different walks of life develop in a comfortable, natural manner. Here, local club members can meet cyclists from other communities and perhaps even from other countries, and share in simple living on overnight stays while touring. The AYH is a good source of ideas for your club program.

Bike clubs in every town vary, depending on the community, the resources and facilities available and the interests of the members. Because of this, it is impossible to set down any rigid blueprint for a club to follow in getting organized. There is only one rule—to be effective a club should satisfy most of its members. Beyond that, the club will have to find its own direction and develop in its own way. Your club, for example, may be interested mainly in racing during the first year. The following year, if an AYH hostel should be established within cycling distance (perhaps through your club's suggestion), your activities may center around hosteling. As the interests of your members change, your activities should change, so be prepared to be flexible.

HOW TO CARRY OUT A BIKE PROGRAM

Once you have decided on a program, you will want to know how to carry out the activities you have planned. Why don't you start with a race meet? This event has several advantages. It will attract community attention—and probably new members—to your club and it will give you an opportunity to get your feet wet. You will learn how to run off races, how to enlist the cooperation of police and other community officials and how to obtain publicity for your club.

Planning a Race Meet

First, locate a racing area. You can use a dirt track or an athletic field, a quiet street, even a fairground. Of course, if you use a street, you will have to get permission from the police department. Chances are, the police will rope off the street and assign one or two men to be present on the day of the meet.

Publicity is very important. If you want your club to grow and to be well-known in the community, the more publicity you obtain, the better. One idea is to mimeograph some flyers giving the time, the place and other details on the meet. Mail these flyers to newspapers, TV and radio stations, and to city, school and civic officials. You can also make up some attractive posters for use on bulletin boards and in store windows. If your race is a fairly large event, ask your local paper to send a sports reporter to cover it.

Now you are ready to plan the races you are going to include and to set up procedures for running them off. After the rules for each event have been established, appoint judges, timers and starters. You may want to present awards or prizes to the winning contestants. Approach the owners of bicycle stores or hardware stores and ask them if they would be interested in giving bike accessories to the winners. In return, you will publicize the stores for presenting the awards.

There are many types of races and other events from which you can choose in selecting a program for your race meet. The simplest race, and the easiest to run off, is the sprint. It is described on page 28. For all short races, use a stop watch and time each cyclist individually. You may want to establish handicaps in relays or straight races if the participating cyclists are of widely varying abilities. There are many ways to work out a handicap. For example, the handicapped team or contestant can start off 100 yards ahead of the faster one. You will have to spend quite a lot of time planning details.

There are many races which are more elaborate than the sprint. What about including a 10-mile relay race? The first cyclist on each team rides $\frac{1}{2}$ mile carrying a baton or small stick; he passes it to the next cyclist on his team and so on. The baton is not even necessary; the racers can simply tag each other. Any relay can be adjusted for different numbers of racers and for different distances. In the 10-mile there can be as many as 20 on each team, but you can run off a 5-mile relay, for instance, with five cyclists on each team. The most important fact about relays is that they are more exciting and more competitive when opposing cyclists are fairly well matched in ability. You should always station the fastest member of each team in the final position.

In the next section you will find a wide variety of races and bike

Outdoor track race, conducted by the Amateur Bicycle League of America. Winners eventually are selected for Olympic tryouts.

events described. Nearly all of them can be adapted to your track and to the distances and number of cyclists you are working with. A word of caution, however: stay away from the dead-heat type of race. This is for extremely experienced racers and requires special equipment such as crash helmets.

Now you're ready! The track has been laid out, the publicity organized and the events planned. Cross your fingers for a sunny day!

CIVIC EVENTS

You can boost your club's prestige in the community by taking part in civic events and parades—watch especially for the Fourth of July, Memorial Day and Veterans' Day. Several weeks before the celebration, go to the chairman of the parade committee with your suggestions. Chances are, he'll be more than happy to let your club participate. Don't let him down, however. Plan your events very carefully so that you will know exactly what equipment each member will need to bring on the day of the parade and the amount of time required for preparation.

A good stunt is to have several cyclists carry a float. This gives a parade dash and color. An interesting touch will be provided if you weave colored crepe paper through the spokes of your wheels. If you can obtain enough of them, tandems and old-fashioned high wheelers are sure to draw attention. If the civic event is in the nature of a field day, you can hold a high wheeler or a tandem race—excellent for fun and laughs! This might also be a good opportunity to stage some of the rodeo games described on pages 17-29.

Supervised bike programs for local clubs and individual cyclists are held annually by more than 250 city recreation departments throughout the United States. Watch for annual sports days sponsored by your local recreation department. Be sure your bike club takes part.

Having Fun with Your Bike

BIKE RODEO

How about organizing a bike rodeo? Like a race meet, a bike rodeo will help you arouse public interest in your club's activities, gain notice in your local newspaper and even add funds to your treasury. You can charge a small admission fee. No matter how you go about planning a bike rodeo, remember that having fun is your real goal.

The rodeo games described here are exciting and challenging and, fortunately, they do not require elaborate preparation. The fewer arrangements you have to make, the easier it will be to plan the games. First, you should decide which of the bike events to include and when and how to run them off. Then obtain a permit from the police or parks department to set aside a street or an area in a city park that has a roadway or cinder path suitable for racing. If you can find an unused area or a black topped schoolyard that is easily reached and for which no permit is necessary, all the better.

You can play any of the games described in this section at any time and, of course, you can make up your own scoring systems. When scheduled for a bike rodeo, however, these events should be scored as follows: If six people are competing, the winner receives 6 points; the remaining five contestants receive 5, 4, 3, 2, 1 points according to their positions. For relays, in which contestants are divided into two groups, scoring is different. If there are three on a team, *each* member of the winning team receives 6 points. This puts a premium on the relay and makes it an especially exciting event.

If your rodeo is organized so that two teams or clubs oppose each other in every event, score each individual separately. At the end of the day, add the individual scores for each side. You will end up with two total team scores. Always base the maximum number of possible points on the number of contestants. For example, if there are twenty entrants, the winner of an event receives 20 points.

You will find it easy to set up and run off these rodeo games. Let's start with three chalk-line games. Find an area at least 100′ × 30′. It should be concrete or something similar so that the chalk will be visible. Let's play Parallel and Slalom.

PARALLEL

For the Parallel you will need 4 feet of string and a few sticks of white chalk.

Draw two parallel lines 75 feet long and 3 feet apart. This can be done by cutting off 3½ feet of string and tying a stick of chalk to each end. Two people take the chalk, one at each end of the string, and walk in a straight line, drawing chalk lines on the ground while keeping the string taut. This method will produce parallel lines. One end is then marked "start"—the other "finish." A contestant who touches a line is disqualified.

Once your course is marked, you can use it for two races—a dash and a slow race. Watch the fun when entrants try to pedal as slowly as possible and still avoid the white lines!

SLALOM

For this race you will need 25 feet of string and a few sticks of white chalk.

The Slalom is named and taken from a famous skiing event in which racers follow a zigzag course down a hill. In the bike Slalom, the cyclist follows a course marked by two parallel zigzag chalk lines on a pavement. Prepare the Slalom by cutting a string $5\frac{1}{2}$ feet long and tying a stick of chalk to each end. The lines are to be 5 feet apart. As for the Parallel, two people draw lines with a stick of chalk, while both hold the

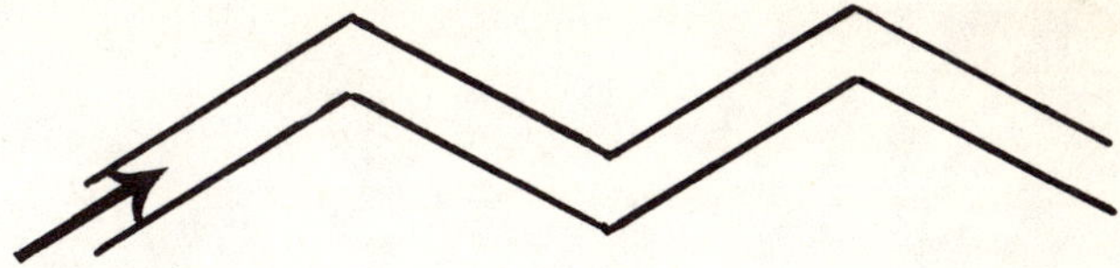

string taut between them. Draw the lines parallel for 20 feet in one direction, then turn and go 20 feet in the other direction. The turn should be approximately 110 degrees, a little wider than a right-angle turn. Make as many turns as you have space for; generally four or five are the maximum. Naturally, the "start" and "finish" are marked at opposite ends.

Each cyclist is timed as he rides down and back the 5-foot-wide course. He is disqualified if he touches the lines or if his foot touches the ground. As in the Parallel event, you can run both fast and slow races.

CIRCLE

For the Circle you will need a pencil, a stick of chalk and 15 feet of string.

Prepare the game by tying a stick of chalk to one end of a 15-foot piece of string and a pencil to the other end. This is how the spiral

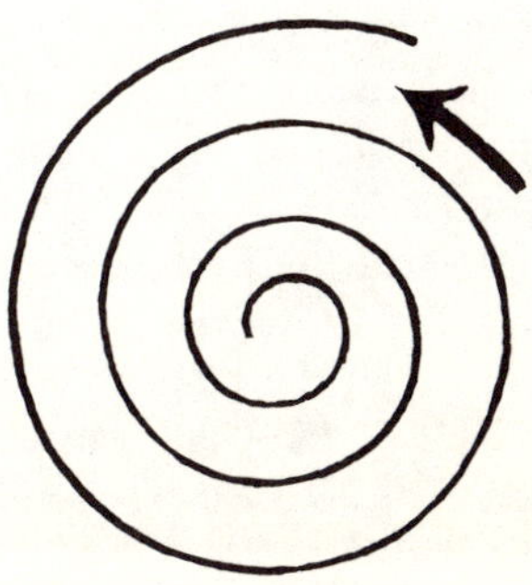

How to lay out the spiral for the "Circle" event.

course is drawn: one person holds the pencil firmly in the center of the pavement while another, holding the string taut, walks in a circle around the man in the center. The person with the pencil-end gradually pulls in the string as his companion circles, thereby lessening the circumference on each round. In this way, a spiral course is automatically drawn, winding from the outer rim inward to the center, where the person with the pencil is standing. There should be 3 or 4 feet separating each inner circle.

You can use your spiral course for both fast and slow races. Time each entrant with a stop watch. As in the preceding two chalk games, a contestant is disqualified if he touches a line. Place the "start" at the opening of the outer circle; the "finish" at the center.

This is the most difficult of the chalk games, for it requires great control and co-ordination. The cyclist must operate his bike as perfectly as if it were a part of his body.

The contestant in "Circle" rides the spiral course from the outer lane to the center, trying not to touch any lines.

SEESAW

You will need one large brick and one plank of wood 18″ wide × 12′ long.

You can plan this simple event as part of a cross-country race, or you can set it up by itself as a demonstration event. Place a brick midway under a plank of wood about 18 inches wide and 12 feet long. The entrant rides up one end of the plank. When he gets just past the center, the other end of the plank suddenly slams down. The cyclist must be ready for this quick change of position. Otherwise he will find himself off-balance and off-bike.

The "Obstacle Drop" is a fine way to develop accuracy and speed on a bike — and it's fun besides.

OBSTACLE DROP

You will need 4 bushel baskets and 4 old tennis balls or rubber balls the same size as tennis balls. Place the bushel baskets open end up in a straight line, about 15 feet apart on a pavement or some other level area. The cyclist attempts to drop one ball into each basket as he weaves around each one in order.

The "start" should be about 20 feet in front of the first basket; the "finish" about 20 feet behind the last basket. This event is timed with a stop watch, and only one entrant competes at a time. The cyclist who places balls in the most baskets in the shortest length of time wins.

For example, a player who gets balls in three baskets will win over one placing balls in only two; if there is a tie, with two or more players having the same number of baskets, the one with the fastest time wins.

Remember that there are two objects to the game: accuracy and speed. If either has to be sacrificed, it should be speed. Practice handling a bike around the baskets; eventually you will develop enough skill to pitch or drop the balls into the baskets from almost any position.

TARGET

You will need 6 large empty cans (each at least 6″ in diameter) and 50 marbles.

Along a course 100 feet long, set the empty cans about 15 feet apart in a straight line. If the ground is soft, press the cans down with the open ends up. Of course, don't destroy grass or gardens to build your gamesite.

After the targets are in place, give each player as many marbles as there are cans. The object of the game is to ride down the course at average speed, dropping one marble into each can. After every run, hits and misses are counted.

You can run off this stunt for any number of rounds. Zooming in on the cans while riding takes skillful timing and marksmanship. But after a few tries you will be able to hit your targets with accuracy.

RING TOSS

You will need 12 rubber jar rings, a 28″-square board and 23 nails, each 3″ long.

Prepare the board by driving the nails partway into it. Distribute the nails as evenly as possible, about 2 inches apart. Now, hang the board on a tree. It should be about 5 feet from the ground.

Each contestant holds 4 jar rings and rides slowly up to the board. The object, of course, is to ring as many nails as possible, and entrants can begin tossing at any distance from the board. Let each player have several runs before you count up his total score.

This is a game for expert cyclists. Because the player rides slowly, he has to keep one hand on the handle bars for steering and balancing.

He must keep the bike under complete control so he can get a clean shot at the board.

BRAKING WITHOUT SKIDDING

All you will need is a piece of chalk.

Set off a 100-foot straightaway and draw a chalk line at about the 75-foot mark. Each rider works up speed till he reaches the chalk line and then brakes, attempting not to skid. If he brakes *before* he reaches the chalk line, he is disqualified. The cyclist who stops within the shortest distance beyond the chalk line without skidding places first; the one who stops within the next shortest distance is second, and so on. Run off the players separately. In this way, the judges can give full attention to skidding, and it will be easy to tell whether the cyclist applied his brake *at* the chalk line, not before.

It is usually left to the judges or other participants to decide whether a cyclist built up sufficient speed to deserve a second chance. An entrant who skids is also given another try, but no more than one extra chance should be allowed any player, or the game will proceed too slowly. If you enter this event, practice braking beforehand.

RELAY

This event is similar to a running-track relay. Six or more entrants can participate in this game, three on a team. After you choose sides the players on the same team line up 100 feet from each other and about 15 feet opposite the competing team. Each side has only one bicycle. If the total relay distance is 300 feet and there are three players on each side, the straightaway or oval track should be divided into three parts of 100 feet each. The roadway should be at least 30 feet wide.

Each person waits at his mark for his teammate. Suppose you are the lead-off man. At the signal, race to the second cyclist on your team and dismount. The second cyclist mounts, rides to the third man and so on, until the last man finishes the relay.

Be sure to mark all positions clearly. You can use a paper tape at the finish line where the judges stand. Two additional watchers should be assigned to stand near where the players on each team mount and dismount.

The keys to mastery of the team bike relay are timing and teamwork in jumping on and off.

You will have to practice often before you master racing in relay. Concentrate on timing and teamwork in jumping on and off. These are the keys to winning any relay.

LEMON RELAY

For this game you will need 2 lemons, 2 tablespoons, and the ability to cycle with one hand. Divide your group into two equal teams, with each team lined up in single file. The two lines of teams should be at least 20 feet apart. Set a marker 100 feet in front of the first cyclist on each team.

At the signal the first cyclist on each team mounts his bike holding the spoon with the lemon in one hand. Suppose you have to lead off.

Ride to the marker 100 feet away, turn around and ride back. Give the spoon (with the lemon still in it) to the next player, who repeats the same ride. If the lemon falls off the spoon, the rider must dismount, replace the lemon and go on from where he is. The relay continues until the last player has completed the run. Of course, the first team to finish the relay wins.

With relatively unskilled cyclists you may have to vary this game. If it becomes too difficult to pass the spoon to the next cyclist while you are on your bike, then dismount when you complete your run. Pass the spoon and lemon while you are standing on the ground.

Silly as it may sound, this game is no "lemon." As well as improving your co-ordination, it will give you plenty of laughs.

CLOTHESLINE RELAY

For this game you need a piece of clothesline about 15 feet long and two clothespins. If you can find two trees the right distance apart, tie each end of the clothesline around the trunk of a tree. If this isn't possible, drive two poles into the ground and tie one end of the rope around each pole. The clothesline should be shoulder high to most of the players.

Divide the group into two teams and have the players line up at right angles to the rope. The teams should be 3 feet apart with the first player on each team about 50 feet from the clothesline. All contestants should be in position to mount their bikes as quickly as possible.

Give the first player on each team a clothespin. At the signal, he hops on his bike, rides to the clothesline, puts the pin on the line, and dashes back to the next player on his team. The second player on each team rides to the clothesline, takes off the pin and rides back to give it to the next player in line, who puts the pin back on the clothesline.

This procedure continues until all players have had their turn. Contestants are not permitted to get off their bikes and when each finishes his turn, he rides to the last position on his team.

Of course, the first team to finish wins.

BICYCLE LETTERS

Here's a novel game you can play to improve your powers of observation.

First, plan a route over a square block or any area that includes a variety of things to be seen. The route should not be longer than 2 miles.

The object of the game is to look for and to remember anything you see beginning with the following letters: B-I-K-E. The objects have to be nouns, for example:

B—bird, bus, bike, branch, bee, etc.

I—iris, illustration, initials, insect, etc.

K—kids, kerchief, kite, kitty, knee, etc.

E—earth, engine, eyes, estuary, elm, etc.

Start out in single file and do not dismount during the entire game. When you see an object beginning with one of the letters in "bike," call out the letter but not the name of the object. Try not to look at the object, or you will tip off the others. When you have called out all the letters spelling "bike" (that is, after you have seen something beginning with B, then I, then K and finally E), yell "bike" and race back to the starting place. The others continue until each has completed the game.

When you are all together, list what you have seen. If some don't believe you have seen what you claim to have observed, they can challenge you to prove it. The winner is the cyclist who has seen the right objects in the shortest period of time.

After the word "bike" select another word related to cycling. It might be the brand name of a bicycle, for instance. But whatever it is, the letters B-I-K-E should not be repeated. Make the game as challenging as you possibly can.

BALLOON MAZE

You will need a piece of chalk and about 20 balloons. This game can only be played on a calm, windless day.

Black top school areas or large driveways are ideal, but if neither is available, chalk off either a circle or a rectangle approximately 30 square feet in area. This will accommodate from four to seven cyclists, but, of course, you can adjust the size of the game area and the number of balloons to the number of players. If you have fewer than four players in a 30-foot area, the game will be too easy. Now, blow up the balloons and place them in the chalked-off space.

The object of the game is for each rider to weave in and out around the balloons without losing his balance and falling, or breaking a balloon. You will have to station someone outside the ring to toss back the balloons if they are knocked out.

Since this is a game which emphasizes skill rather than competitiveness, you can keep your own score; each time you touch the ground with your foot or break a balloon one point is counted against you. Naturally, the player with the lowest score after all the balloons are broken or after a definite prearranged length of time is the winner. Fifteen minutes is a good time limit.

The Balloon Maze demands tremendous cycling skill! You have to avoid both the balloons and the other riders—all the while keeping your balance!

SPRINT

The simplest event to arrange and perform is the sprint or fast race. You need a protected straightaway or oval track of 500 to 1000 feet. It should be at least 30 feet wide. All entrants can make the dash simultaneously, or if the track is narrow or the group inexperienced, the race can be run off with two entrants at a time competing in an elimination contest. Each judge should watch one cyclist only, to determine accurately his place at the tape.

The sprint requires strength, energy, and easy bike acceleration. But you do not have to be an expert cyclist, or own a racer, to participate in it. Although a racer or a lightweight bike is best for the sprint, it is by no means a requirement. Anyone can enjoy a brisk race!

"On your mark, get ready — go!" The sprint is an exciting event for participants and spectators alike.

COASTING RACE

Test your skill and your bike's ability to coast. For this race your cycle must be in top shape—cleaned, oiled, and stripped of extra equipment.

Select either a level straightaway, or one that starts out by being level and then rises gradually into an incline.

At the signal, pedal as fast as you can. At a predetermined point, marked by a flag, stop pedaling. Coast to the finish line.

Now, check the coasting distance of each bike. The longest coaster wins. Remember to station a judge at the point at which racers must stop pedaling.

You can run off this race several times so that each contestant can have a chance to improve his own record.

BUILDING A BIKE PATH

In many cities, bikeways—routes composed of streets and secondary roads which have a minimum of traffic and are marked with signs for bicyclists—have been developed. They are creating much appeal for the cyclist who wants a more protected, scenic, and uncluttered ride. If your bike club is interested in constructing bikeways in your city, consult with your schools, local newspapers, service organizations, civic clubs and the city planning director to mobilize support for your project. A guide to the design and construction of bicycle paths, *Bike Trails and Facilities*, can be obtained from the American Institute of Park Executives, Oglebay Park, Wheeling, West Virginia.

CROSS-COUNTRY

You will enjoy marking out this course for yourself. Plan the race over natural inclines, bridges, creeks, woods and parks. One cross-country event we planned called on the racers to ford a creek, climb a hill, cross a bridge, ride through a thicket and dash the last 300 feet to the finish line. You should include as many natural obstacles as possible, but exactly which ones you use will depend on the topography in the area of your home. If you think it is necessary, you can invent your own obstacles. For example, cinders and loose earth can be piled up to make an interesting incline or a steep bank on a curve.

Although spectators see only a small part of a cross-country race, usually the end of the sprint, as a participant you will find the cross-country packed with thrills and adventures. Remember, though, that all the entrants should be taken over the course by a judge before the event begins. Everyone should be aware of the course and of its obstacles. Emphasize the interest rather than the difficulty of the race. There should not be too many large rocks in the streams you ford, and trails leading between trees should be wide enough for safety.

Use care in planning your cross-country course. It is a free-for-all, but it should not be dangerous.

This cross-country race begins with fording a creek, then there might be a hill to climb and a bridge to cross. If there are no natural obstacles in your neighborhood, you can create some.

Above: There's no time to stop and rest, so endurance is all-important in the cross-country race.

Below: Even though you'll be anxious to complete the course, you can still enjoy the scenery on the way.

Above: **A woody thicket presents a challenging obstacle, but the finish line is just ahead.**

Below: **The winner! After the sprint to the finish line the tape is broken. Tired but proud, the victorious rider can now collect his prize.**

HILL CLIMB

This event is modeled on a famous motorcycle race, but it is much less dangerous. The idea is to climb a steep hill with all the speed you can muster. You must choose a hill with enough straightaway leading up to it for the racers to build up speed. The steeper it is, the shorter it should be. Although you will want a challenging course, it must not be too difficult to negotiate.

You may have to search for just the right hill. Investigate nearby schools and parks, but stay away from embankments near highways. These are dangerous. Once you think you have found the right hill, give it a test climb.

It is best to run off the contestants individually to avoid possible collisions. And, of course, you will need a stop watch with a second hand. On your mark!

NEWSPAPER RACE

It's natural to associate boys and bicycles with newspapers—so why not have a newspaper race? Sailing folded papers at a given target is always fun.

For this game you will need 2 upright poles, a wooden stake for a marker, an old blanket or sheet and 2 newspapers per player.

To prepare the event, tack the blanket or sheet to the upright poles—more simply, just drape the blanket over a low-hanging branch. The blanket is your target—big enough to see and big enough to hit—that is, if you're in good hurling shape. Thirty feet in front of the target, set a marker in the ground.

To fold the paper the way the newsboys do, first fold a complete section in half. Now, roll it horizontally and tuck in both ends. Remember, each player should have two folded papers.

With a paper under each arm, the contestant starts at a point 100 feet away from the target and rides toward the marker set 30 feet in front of the target. The cyclist must throw both papers *before* he reaches this marker.

A single hit is worth 1 point; two hits will earn 2 points. The game continues until someone accumulates 10 points.

OTHER GAMES AND TESTS OF SKILL

Although race meets and rodeos are wonderful fun, you do not have to compete with others to enjoy riding your bike. Ever try competing with yourself? You can play many of the bike rodeo games alone. Test yourself on an event (say, Bike Balance described below); run through it again. Did your performance improve? Now, try it again—and again. Challenge yourself; this is an excellent way to improve your skill in handling a bicycle.

Some games emphasize riding skills less than mental ones. Unlike the rodeo games, most of the following games emphasize powers of observation and quick thinking. These games, too, are meant to be played while you are riding your bike. For example, Bike Geography, described on page 38, is an especially good game for touring or cross-country trips. It can be played by two or more cyclists.

The important thing to remember about *all* bike games is that they are adaptable. You can play many alone, against other contestants or even in teams. Test your ingenuity. You may be able to invent some games of your own!

BIKE BALANCE

Did you ever try to walk balancing a book on your head? It's easy, you say? Then try it while riding your bike!

The object of the game is to see how far you can ride before the book topples off. It's hard, but with a little practice you can master this balancing feat.

To warm up for this stunt, try walking with the book on your head. Then, when you become quite proficient, try it on your bike. Use a book you don't want any more; frequent falls will damage the binding.

This doesn't have to be a competitive event, but just a game of skill. Try it. You'll be surprised at the improvement in your posture.

SCAVENGER HUNT

You will have to plan this game in advance, but even that will be fun —you will be doing it on your bike!

First, lay out a course from ½ to 3 miles long, depending on how extensive you want the hunt to be. It will be easier and more fun if you take along a friend. While you are establishing the course, make a list of things you want the players to observe or discover. Here are some examples of how you should set up the instructions for the hunt:

Ride down Elm Street.

How many fire plugs are there between Maple and Wood Streets?

Continue to First Ave.

How many different items are in Wolfe's drug store window?

Turn right and come back by way of Second Ave. There are two initials on a lamppost on Second near Wood. What are the initials?

On Fern Lane there is a doghouse.

What color is it?

Continue your list of instructions with the final question designed to bring the scavengers back to the starting point.

Make your list of questions in triplicate so that each team will have a list, and you should keep a master copy noting the answers. One person on each team keeps the list and writes down the answers underneath each question. To make things easier, have one team start the route from the beginning, and the other work backward from the last instruction to the first one. This will eliminate confusion and crowding during the hunt.

The first team to finish with the greatest number of correct answers wins.

BIKE POLO

This is a fast, energetic sport for two teams. Played from a bicycle saddle, the "sport of princes" is too young to have become part of the athletic tradition of the United States, but it is played enthusiastically in the eastern states. There are many bicycle-polo clubs in England and in Europe where this comparatively new sport is extremely popular.

The game is quite simple. It is played on a level field about 175 yards long and 75 yards wide, with a goal at each end, marked by posts 12 feet

Bike Polo is a fast, rough and tumble battle that has long been popular in England, and is rapidly gaining enthusiastic followers in the United States. Here the Grand Prix of the London polo tournament is being decided at Mitcham Football Ground.

apart. You can use actual polo fields or football fields, if they are smooth enough.

The four players on each team attempt to hit a wooden polo ball through the opposing goal. Each player has a polo mallet 32 inches long, and a helmet for protection. There are four basic strokes: forehand and backhand with the right hand, and forehand and backhand with the left hand. Lightweight bikes with gear shifts are best for this game. Naturally, bike polo requires a great amount of team play, practice and facility with a bike. But, your effort will be rewarded. Few sports are as exciting as bike polo.

BIKE GEOGRAPHY

This game is wonderful for trips. It can be played while you are riding in single file formation, or while you are resting.

The first cyclist starts by calling out the name of any city in the world: for example, Portland. The next in line has to answer with the name of a city beginning with the last letter in Portland. That could be Denver. The third cyclist answers with Rangoon, and so forth until the last in line has had his turn. Then you can begin again with the first player.

If a cyclist cannot think of a name in a reasonable period of time, say 10 seconds, he receives one demerit. If he gets 3 demerits, he is eliminated. If timing is a problem, the group can count to 10 together. After the count of 10 the player must call out his answer. Make your answers loud and clear so that everyone can hear.

Trips and Tours

HOW TO PLAN A TRIP

Planning a trip in advance will make it easier and more fun. First, decide whether you want to go alone or with a group. Chances are, you will want company. Touring is more interesting when you can share your impressions and experiences with others. So your group should first agree on what it most wants from the trip—just a good ride, a swim in a nearby lake, a visit to an historical site, or hosteling. Once this has been decided, you are ready to lay out your course.

What sort of route will your group choose? Some cyclists enjoy taking main highways; others prefer side roads and byways. In fact, inexperienced riders should use relatively untraveled roads so that they can build up "bike legs" and develop a feeling of security in traffic. In planning your route, you will want to refer to maps. The easiest maps to obtain are those printed by oil companies or auto clubs, but you can also get detailed contour maps of almost any area in the United States for 50 cents apiece by writing to your State Department of Conservation or to the U.S. Geological Survey in Washington, D.C.

Group travel is sometimes difficult unless riders are of approximately the same riding ability. Fast cyclists have a lonely time of it way up ahead, and beginners feel left out and discouraged if they find themselves hanging far behind the others. If your group has this problem, you may be able to get some of the faster members to take a rest now and then to wait for the others. Another suggestion is to divide the group according to cycling abilities. Assign a leader to "pace" each group.

After you have decided on your route, try to talk to other bike enthusiasts who have taken the same trip. Map information is invaluable, but it is a good idea to supplement it whenever possible with the advice of someone who knows the route. You can find out which are the best roads, the location of the most scenic areas, the best lakes and rivers for swimming, what spots of historical interest are along the way and where your group can find tourist homes or hostels. It's particularly important to get personal information if you plan to camp overnight.

You can keep your own touring records quite easily. Just ask each club member to write a brief report giving his impressions of the trip and all data he thinks would be valuable to a cyclist who had never before been over the route. Collect these reports. Whether you file them or keep them in a scrapbook, they will become a valuable part of your club records.

Once you've decided when and where you're going, set a starting time and place. Make sure all members of the tour have this information. Now, you're all set! If your planning was thorough, you're bound to have a wonderful trip!

LOCAL TRIPS

Local trips are those planned for distances under 20 miles, round trip. Remember that if you live in a relatively flat rural area, your traveling time will be different from what it would be in an urban area. You can cover the same amount of ground in the country in less time than in the city. You will want to adjust the length of the trip to suit traffic and geographical conditions.

Local trips can be very exciting, but their secondary purpose is to get you in shape for longer tours. You will probably select for your destination an historical, geographical or cultural point of interest in or near your community. For example, city cyclists may want to visit homes of famous people, unusual buildings, zoos, museums, aquariums, parks, canals, rivers or bridges. Most parks, zoos and college or university campuses are crisscrossed with lanes and paths, making it quite easy for you to travel on your bike, observing the scenery. Of course, if you see signs prohibiting bicycles, you will observe them and you will remember to give pedestrians the right of way.

If you live in a small town or in the country, there are probably so

Every part of the country has something to offer. Here, a couple on a tandem are enjoying the countryside.

many places to visit that you will have a hard time making a choice. Think of it—endless scenic areas, lakes, rock formations, dams, hills, surrounding villages. You can plan an outing, a picnic, a swimming activity—and you can hold it in any one of many lovely spots!

PRACTICE TRIPS

The purpose of a practice trip is to get you in shape for a longer one. If you plan a tour longer than 15 miles, certainly you should take a practice trip first. Here is a simple ratio for establishing the length of a practice trip: the ratio is 3-1. For example, if you are training for a tour of 30 miles, your preliminary trip should cover 10 miles of terrain as similar as possible to that of the longer trip.

If you are not a member of a bike club, get a friend to go along; companionship always adds to the fun of cycling.

You'll be wise to practice carrying exactly the same equipment you plan to use on your big journey. This will help give you an accurate measure of your endurance. Here are some other suggestions for practice trips: start early in the morning, so you will be back by dark. If the weather becomes hot and humid, shorten the distance you plan to cover and take many rest breaks. (Generally you should rest 10 to 15 minutes every hour.) Try to stop in shady areas. Stretch out on the grass. Relax. If you are thirsty, take some water. Have a snack of cheese and crackers or fresh fruit.

The second purpose of a practice trip is to give you an idea of your cycling ability and endurance. Naturally, these are different for different people. Some can do 10 hilly miles a day, others only 5. Some find that they have to avoid hills altogether. This is the sort of thing you will discover on a practice trip, providing you keep a record of the distance traveled, the type of terrain and the time taken by the trip from start to finish. By dividing your traveling time into the mileage covered, you will know whether you average 6 or 8 miles an hour, for instance, under certain specific conditions. Suppose that in 3 hours you covered 15 miles over a flat, slightly rolling road; then your average rate of travel is 5 miles an hour. If you don't have a speedometer to take with you, you can find out what mileage you covered from a map or from your local auto club.

Don't be discouraged if you discover that you need more than one practice trip to put you in good shape for a tour. This is not unusual. You haven't lost a thing. Practice trips are just as much fun as more rigorous ones!

WHAT IS HOSTELING?

You must be wondering when you will be ready to take an overnight trip. You've got yourself in good physical condition; you've been on at least one practice trip and you know your average cycling speed. Just one thing more before you plan an overnight trip—you should be introduced to American Youth Hostels, Inc.

The AYH is fairly new in this country and not as well known as it should be. In 1934 two American schoolteachers, Monroe and Isabel Smith, introduced hostels in the United States. While making a survey of youth organizations, the Smiths observed the European hostel movement. They saw many people, both young and old, enjoying the outdoors and becoming acquainted with their own and with other countries by hiking or cycling. To the Smiths, hostelers seemed to have "a practical understanding and appreciation of nature and how people live."

They determined to bring hosteling to the United States. With great zeal the Smiths set up the first youth hostel in Northfield, Massachusetts. That hostel (or shelter) became the center from which sprang other hostels. Today there are more than 100 hostels in regions all over the country, providing sleeping and cooking accommodations at extremely low rates. Hosteling is probably the least expensive of all ways to travel.

The privilege of joining the AYH and of using hostels is open to anyone of any race, religion or nationality, between the ages of 9 and 90. The only requirement is that you travel under your own steam, that is, by bicycle, canoe, skis or on foot. For membership details, apply to your local AYH council, of which there are 27 in the United States, or to national headquarters, 20 West 17th Street, New York, N.Y. 10011. Membership will entitle you to use any hostel in the world.

In the United States, hostels are sponsored by local groups interested in the movement and in establishing a hostel in their community. Shelters may be in barns, old houses, former Navy barracks, interesting lighthouses, or in similar buildings. Most accommodations are comfortable, and all are clean and supervised.

Sleeping quarters for men and women are separate, but each hostel has a community center where hostelers meet while cooking their meals. Some hostels have game rooms or common lounges equipped with phonographs and radios. There is often space for square dancing.

You will have no trouble meeting fellow hostelers.

Youth Hostel on Nantucket offers warm hospitality at the end of a day of biking.

NOVICE TOURS

Now that you have developed your bike legs on a local trip or practice trip and know about the facilities of the AYH, you are ready for an overnight tour.

Novice tours include 30 to 50 miles of travel over a period of two days. You can camp out, stay at an AYH hostel or rent a room overnight. You and your friends will have to decide before you start out where you are going to stay, what route you will follow and whether maps and train schedules are necessary. In short, you will have to plan all the details of the trip very carefully.

Often, it is convenient to combine modes of transportation. You can save a great deal of time by traveling to your selected touring area by car, bus or train. However, if you use other types of travel for part of your trip, be sure to find out in advance whether you can bring your bicycle along. See page 51. One year we rode from Washington, D.C.,

For quiet and local color, Menemsha Bight, a fishing village on Martha's Vineyard, is unsurpassed.

Cyclists riding through the rain should be equipped with lamps and ponchos.

to Harpers Ferry, West Virginia (with our bikes in the baggage car) and explored this historic spot, taking photographs of ruins from the Civil War period. We stayed overnight and the next day we cycled to Martinsburg, West Virginia, another interesting town. Here, we spent the day touring around and taking pictures. That night we boarded the train returning to Washington.

Another tour took us to the beautiful island of Martha's Vineyard. Starting from Sandwich, Massachusetts, we cycled 20 miles through lovely countryside to Woods Hole. Here we boarded the ferry to Martha's Vineyard, sailing out on the Atlantic Ocean to the port, Vineyard Haven. There we got off and cycled to the youth hostel in West Tisbury. The next day we explored this fascinating island. There were fishing villages, bathing beaches, a lighthouse, intriguing fresh-water ponds, pine forests, cliffs of rainbow hue and many stately early American homes. This was a short trip, but it was rich in things to see and do.

INTERMEDIATE TOURS

These tours last less than a week, involve several overnight stops and an average of 20 to 30 miles between lodgings. You shouldn't attempt this type of tour until you have taken many practice trips, including at least one full-day cycling outing.

It is important that you know your average cycling rate: 10, 20 or 30 miles a day. If you do 25 miles a day, of course you will plan your trip on the basis of this rate. If you're about to take your first long trip, plan conservatively. Figure your daily mileage at slightly less than it usually is. Remember, too, to adjust the distances you think you can cover to the relative hilliness of the terrain. If you get to your destination ahead of schedule, you can always put the extra time to good use. Plan so that you can avoid feeling rushed.

Bike hosteling clubs have sprung up all over the country. Every week-end, clubs like this one in the Potomac area, set out on the open road.

As in planning any other trip, use a detailed map and check any transportation schedules you will use. Try to co-ordinate your travel times so you won't have undesirable long waits between connections. These can be fun if your stopover is in an interesting area; otherwise, you will want to schedule your connections fairly closely. Variety in transportation will give you a relaxing change of pace and will enable you to see more of the country than if you traveled by bike only. See page 51.

If you are not acquainted with the area you're going to cover, try to learn something about the nature of the roads. Find out if they are hilly or flat, if they are in good condition, if they are gravel or paved. Is there heavy traffic? Are there parks and swimming areas? Are there any historical, cultural or scenic points of interest? Will you camp, stay at a youth hostel or at a guest home? These details should be arranged before you set out.

You can get a great deal of information from a map or an American Automobile Association Yearbook. Geography, guide books and travel books will also be helpful in giving you information about the area you want to visit.

Here is a sample trip in Massachusetts and Vermont, suggested by the AYH. The hostels are close together, giving you ample time to visit interesting places.

Springfield, Massachusetts (Springfield College Camp Youth Hostel). Storrowtown, restored colonial village on Eastern States Exposition grounds; swimming; Springfield College; paper mills; Forest Park; wildlife exhibit; Mt. Holyoke College; candlepin bowling; volleyball; softball; boating. Next hostel is 32 miles away.

Sunderland, Massachusetts (Little Meadow Youth Hostel). Trails on Mt. Toby Reservation to waterfall; bicycle museum; antique shops; square dances; sunset from Sugar Loaf; fine swimming in Connecticut River; Old Deerfield; fish hatchery, fire tower. Next hostel is 22 miles away.

Guilford, Vermont (Falls River Youth Hostel). Swimming at Memorial Park in Brattleboro. Sailing on Connecticut River. Next hostel is 23 miles north.

Putney, Vermont (Putney School Youth Hostel). Swimming; Putney School Mountain trails; square dances; Putney School; basket factory.

There are many interesting tours all over the country, and some are much more ambitious than the one just described. Supplemental hostel accommodations (guest houses, "Y's." etc.) can often be arranged in advance through the AYH.

Similar supplemental overnight accommodations frequently are available, for example, along California's Highway 1. This is a tour you can make with a group under AYH leadership. On this trip along the California coastline, you will find hostels in Calistoga, San Francisco, Los Altos, Los Angeles, Pomona, Hemet and San Diego.

On the Atlantic seaboard there is a picturesque tour, rich in Civil War history, from Washington, D.C., to Cumberland, Maryland, a distance of 185 miles. This tour follows the Chesapeake and Ohio Canal, and a chain of hostels is being developed near the towpath once used by horses guiding the canal boats. Every five to eight miles along the towpath are rudimentary camping areas for both walkers and bikers. The camping sites are equipped with drinking water, bathroom facilities and overnight shelters. The National Park Service plans to develop the entire canal as a national park.

You can easily arrange tours in the vicinities of cities that have hostel facilities. Areas around Philadelphia, New York, Boston, Milwaukee, Los Angeles and Detroit all have several hostels.

Remember, though, that you can arrange tours wherever you live—even though there may be no hostel. All you need for a tour is a bike!

THE AMERICAN YOUTH HOSTELS NORTH AMERICAN BIKE ATLAS is an invaluable book of 100 mapped bike rides from coast to coast, a week to a month in duration, covering 47 States, 6 Canadian provinces, Mexico and the Caribbean area. It also includes 60 interesting one day and weekend rides, with routes, sights to see, places to stay, etc. It is compiled by Warren Asa, AYH Western Region Director and has a foreword by Dr. Paul Dudley White. It is the only book of its kind and can be obtained by sending a check or money order to:—

AMERICAN YOUTH HOSTELS, INC.
20 West 17th Street
New York, N.Y. 10011

The cost is $1.50 to members, $1.95 to nonmembers plus 50¢ to cover handling and mailing charges.

ADVANCED TOURS

Tours that are more than one week long, with an average of 25 miles or more between lodgings, are considered advanced. They require a great deal of training and experience. Your body has to be able to take the rigors of the road. You will need stamina and good lung power—both the results of serious practice. Do not undertake an advanced tour unless you are at least 15 years old, and no matter how old you are, don't take a long tour by yourself.

First, select the area you want to visit; list all the points of interest, available swimming facilities, camping, fishing and hiking areas along the way. Determine whether you will use only your bike, or other types of transportation as well.

If you use only your bike, plan to rest for a day or two after two or three days of steady touring. Otherwise, you will get very tired. The rest will refresh you, and also give you ample time to enjoy the country-side, city and whatever sights it has to offer.

The AYH plans and schedules all-expense advanced tours throughout the United States and abroad. A tour leader is assigned to every nine hostelers. For further details, write to AYH, 20 West 17th St., New York, N.Y. 10011.

To give you an idea of how comprehensive an advanced tour can be, here is an itinerary of a sample AYH tour lasting four weeks.

Trip in the Great Lakes Region

Cassapolis is the orientation point where hostelers get acquainted with one another, with AYH procedures, bike safety, menu planning, packing and budgeting. Hostelers take time off for swimming and canoeing before setting out. From here they go to:—

Detroit, Michigan where they visit the Henry Ford Museum and Greenfield Village, Ford Rotunda and the River Rouge plant of the Ford Motor Company, the Detroit Institute of Arts, Belle Isle, the zoological gardens, conservatory and aquarium, the Museum of Great Lakes History, Detroit Zoological Park, Fort Wayne Military Museum, Lake Erie. From here the group cycles to—

Ann Arbor, Michigan, the site of the University of Michigan. The group can cycle, get horses at the riding stables, or hike. From here, they cycle to—

Milford, Michigan, and stay at the Foote Youth Hostel. Here there are sawmills and oil fields to visit, and ghost towns to explore. Horseback riding and swimming are available. From here the group goes about 200 miles to—

Interlochen State Park. Cyclists camp in the Interlochen camping grounds where they may hear the National Music Camp concerts and see the ballets and plays offered each night. Hostelers take a ferry across Lake Michigan to—

Sturgeon Bay, Wisconsin. They can cycle around this resort area, swim in Lake Michigan and Sturgeon Bay, visit cherry orchards and go to the Door County Historical Museum. The next stage is—

Ephraim, Wisconsin. They can attend the Door County Music Festival, the Peninsula Players' Outdoor Theatre, visit Fish Creek and Egg Harbor. There is swimming, canoeing, horseback riding and square dancing, as well as an old lighthouse to visit and, at Sister Bay, a logging mill to explore. From here the tour goes on to—

Washington Island, Wisconsin. Group stays at the Washington Island Youth Hostel. In this area there are cheese factories, mink farms, a museum, a Scandinavian festival, a fishing dock at Jackson Harbor, lovely scenery to view at West Harbor. Pebble Beach is a fine place to swim. From here the cyclists go to—

Two Rivers, Wisconsin. Two Rivers Youth Hostel is the host. There is a Coast Guard Station, a number of fisheries, outdoor band concerts, a lighthouse and Point Beach Park. From here the cyclists go south to—

Greendale, Wisconsin. In nearby *Milwaukee* the cyclists visit the Washington Park Zoo, tour one of the famous breweries, go to Whitehall Park and see exhibits at the Milwaukee Art Institute. From Milwaukee the next stop is—

Racine, Wisconsin. They tour the Johnson wax factory, designed by Wisconsin's famous architect, Frank Lloyd Wright. The cyclists then bike to Wind Point Lighthouse for swimming. From here the tour goes on to—

Chicago, Illinois. This is the terminal city. If the cyclists are not too tired, they can ride for over 15 miles of paved, marked bike paths along the scenic lake front. These paths lead to the major museums of the city, as well as the aquarium and planetarium.

CYCLE TRIPS

Many cyclists, particularly those who live in cities, find it convenient to take a train to the area in which they want to ride. This enables them to avoid uninteresting territory, and to save time.

Some railroads allow you to check your bicycle through to your destination for no extra charge. However, there is one vital precaution! Make sure your train has a baggage car. Then check as to whether you will be permitted to transport your bicycle on this train.

Other railroads may permit you to carry your bike with you onto the coach car, particularly if you can detach the front wheel from the frame so that it occupies less space. Of course, if you have a folding bike it will make it that much easier!

Of course, you can also transport your bike by auto. Just attach it to the back of the car and drive to the desired area. Some cyclists have cars with bike barriers built onto the rear bumper; some install simple toting devices. Other cyclists place their bikes directly on the back

Courtesy Bike Toter, Inc., Box 888, Santa Monica, Calif. 90406.

The Bike Toter can be attached to the rear bumper of almost every car. It will carry one or two fully assembled bikes (three in a pinch), and sells for less than $15.

bumper of the car. Rest the bike upside down on the bumper, then tie the handle bars and seat to the bumper. Now, pull the rope through the door of the luggage compartment and tie the bike firmly against the body of the car. To prevent scratching, put an old blanket between the bike and the car.

OVERSEAS TOURS

One of the finest travel experiences you can have is an overseas tour. Since so many arrangements are necessary, you will probably want to think in terms of a group tour. The best organization for this kind of program is the AYH, particularly if your budget is limited.

Each year the AYH conducts European tours. You will travel with a compatible group of young people, all of whom have important interests in common—cycling, love of travel and of the outdoors. For each group of nine travelers there is a trained leader. The minimum age for overseas touring is 16.

Overseas tours are educational as well as fun. You will get valuable experience in group living and in learning how to get along with others on a day-to-day basis. Compared with other overseas trips, AYH tours are very inexpensive. For example, a thirty-day tour of Europe which includes round-trip jet transportation from New York City to Amsterdam with several incidentals costs $225.

If you sign up for an AYH tour, you will receive a trip forecast giving the main points of interest in various areas. Here is a sample:

Trip Forecast for England, Belgium and the Netherlands

Listed below are towns and cities included in your itinerary with a brief idea of attractions in each area. The group will sightsee, attend festivals, concerts and theatres, depending on group interest and budget. You are expected to help with all aspects of the trip, such as asking directions; shopping for, carrying and preparing food; cleaning up. Hostel regulations require that you do some work for each hostel that you stay in. An average of 35 miles per day will be cycled, using trains and steamers for long distances. Groups will spend approximately 4 days in England, 1 week in Belgium or Holland, 1 week in Germany, 5 days in France, and 1 week in Switzerland. Equipment lists and preparatory bulletins are sent upon application; final itinerary with mail stops will be sent about 4 weeks before departure.

London, England. Modern London is one of the few cities of the world where tradition and historical charm have been graciously combined with the flamboyance of the pop-art Carnaby Street generation. The richness of the English tradition can be seen in the superior museums, Buckingham Palace, Westminster Abbey, the Tower of London, and other historical sights. The modern side of the London scene is in the discotheques and the extravagantly fashionable shops.

Southampton, England (hostel). See old Roman ruins, medieval walls, Tudor House Museum.

Salisbury, England (hostel). Historical abbey, cathedral, quaint thatched cottages, country roads, trip to Stonehenge—Druid ruins.

Shaftesbury, England (hostel). Attractive old market town and health resort. Museum in old abbey grounds.

Cheddar, England (hostel). A picturesque village at the foot of lovely Cheddar Gorge, famous caves. Cycling via Wells—beautiful cathedral with 300 medieval figures around front.

Bath, England (hostel). Oldest spa in Britain, Roman Baths, historic abbey, associations with all the great men of the 18th century.

Duntisbourne Abbots, England (hostel). Early English church containing a Norman font and ancient stone coffin built into the wall of the church.

Broom, England (hostel). Ten miles from Stratford-on-Avon, birthplace of William Shakespeare. New Place Museum and Garden, Anne Hathaway's Cottage, typical tea rooms, walks through countryside, trip to Warwick Castle.

Stow-on-Wold, England (hostel). Lovely cycling through Cotswolds. Ancient market town on hill at northern end of Cotswolds. Has many old buildings, village stocks and market cross.

Oxford, England (hostel). University city founded in the 10th century. Superb architecture of almost every period, beautiful gardens, Bodleian Library, Ashmolean Museum, cathedral, churches and all the colleges.

Henley-on-Thames, England (hostel). Pleasant country town and resort. Henley Royal Regatta draws competitors from all over the world and is one of the social events of the London season. Grey's Court, a 13th-century fortified manor house, is three miles away.

Canterbury, England (hostel). Colorful historic town dating from 597, cathedral with shrine to St. Thomas à Becket, St. Nicholas' Leper Church, city walls, moat, bastions, Roman mosaic pavement.

Dover, England (hostel). White cliffs of Dover, Roman lighthouse, castle, town hall.

The Low Countries. Groups will visit *either* Belgium *or* the Netherlands.

Belgium. Two races are associated to form the Kingdom of Belgium: Flemish and Walloon. The Flemish inhabit the plain and speak a language akin to Dutch. The Walloon dwell in the hilly part of the country and speak French. *Brussels.* Fine parks and wide avenues mark the capital of Belgium. Situated at the border of the Walloon and Flemish parts of the country, Flemish predominates in the lower town and French in the upper. The lower town is very animated, the commercial and artistic center. The upper town is distinguished by the aristocratic atmosphere, parks, official buildings. *Bruges.* A Medieval city built on canals. *Antwerp.* Port city with beautiful Gothic and Renaissance buildings. Diamond cutting center and site of a Rubens museum.

Netherlands. Country of vast horizons, bouquets of trees, and reflections in the water. *Amsterdam.* Called the "Venice of the North," the main part of Amsterdam has rings of canals which were once the principal means of transportation. As it was for many years the largest port of the Dutch Empire, there are many Indonesian restaurants and shops. While sightseeing, you will want to visit the home of Rembrandt and the Modern Art Museum (Stedelijkmuseum) which houses many Van Gogh paintings. *Amersfoort.* Garden city with the Koppelpoort, 15th century watergate on the river Ems.

Rotterdam, Netherlands (hostel). Largest port in Europe, rebuilt since the war with much modern architecture. Boyman's Museum, town hall, Waalhaven Dock, wholesalers' building and one of Europe's best zoos.

The Hague, Netherlands (hostel). Seat of government, residence of Queen, home of International Court of Justice. Visit Binnenhof (Parliament buildings, Hall of Knights, Throne Room), art gallery with Hals, Rubens, Vermeer, and Holbein paintings, Peace Palace, Spinoza House, Vijver, and Madurodam (miniature city).

Bonn, Germany. Rhine steamer past the Lorelei Rock to Beethoven's

A cycling tour of a foreign country is the goal of many biking enthusiasts. Bike riding provides an unequalled opportunity to meet the people of towns and villages.

birthplace and capital of West Germany. See the Government buildings, Beethoven's house and museum, the University and Zoological Museum with its famous animal collection. *Cologne*. Magnificent Gothic cathedral and dancing in the Rhine river park. *Rhine River Towns*. Relax aboard a steamer heading up the Rhine past castles, the vineyards, and tiny villages. The Rhine is a main artery of transportation and cuts through beautiful countryside. *Heidelberg*. University city and splendid setting. Castle dominates the town. Go to the students' inns and prisons. Dine at student restaurants with fencing decor.

Strasbourg, France. Ancient city in Alsace where the people are not really German and not really French, but Alsatians first. The old section of the city, "La Petite France" is a maze of tiny streets lined with small restaurants and bistros; also the cathedral, Chateau de Rohan, and the port. From here you will cycle south through the wine

Cycling through Europe is an inexpensive way to make the Grand Tour. Here bikes are unloaded from the boat train in Paris.

country along the Rhine. Winding roads through vineyards, and sloping hills. *Selestat.* Nearby is the castle Haut Koenigsburg, with high turrets, ramparts, spooky fogs; built to defend the area from invaders across the Rhine.

Lucerne, Switzerland is situated on the north west tip of Lake Lucerne, with summer festivals, chapel bridge, and Swiss watches. *Interlaken.* Health and pleasure resort located in a majestic valley dominated by the Jungfrau. *Gimmelvald-Murren.* Alpine skiing and climbing areas near the Matterhorn. Snow covered peaks, white glaciers and green mountain fields. *Bern.* Capital with a pleasant blend of fine traditional past and the features of modern life. Visit the arcades, Tobler chocolate factory and the bear pits.

**For those on the* 60 *day version of this trip,* the group will disband here for 30 days of independent travel at the trippers' own expense. The group will re-unite in Amsterdam for the flight back to the U.S.

**For those on the August Special version of this trip* with only 4 weeks in Europe, the group will proceed directly to Amsterdam from Bern for the flight back to the U.S.

Groups depart from New York for Europe by sea or air in June, July and August. The AYH schedules tours to 18 European countries, Mexico and Japan. Trips last from 4 to 16 weeks.

A four week trip to Mexico via station wagon and public transportation is listed at $565. It includes everything interesting in California from redwood forests and the Monterey peninsula to the vacation thrills of Mexico, such as the native markets, the pyramids, the archeological remains and the Gulf of Mexico.

HOW TO PREPARE FOR TOURING

Now that you know what kinds of tours your club can arrange, from short local excursions to extremely advanced European trips, you are probably anxious to pack and get started. But wait a minute! The surest way to spoil a tour is to set out before you are thoroughly prepared.

While touring, your bike is your "home," and you will have to know how to live safely and comfortably "on the road." Select the proper equipment and clothing and learn to protect yourself from illness and injuries—these are just two of the many things you must do before you can safely set out on a tour.

First of all, you must get yourself into excellent physical condition.

GETTING INTO CONDITION FOR YOUR TRIP

On page 41 you learned the importance of practicing in preparation for longer trips. But there is much more to preparation than riding.

For extended bike trips you must be in good physical condition. When you ride a bike, you are not a rider only. You are the engine as well. Your physical condition will determine how fast you can travel and how far you can go.

A strong body needs good food. You should drink at least three glasses of milk every day. You should eat one green and one yellow vegetable daily, and plenty of protein foods such as meat, fish, eggs and cheese. Fresh fruits, whole wheat bread and natural cereals are also essential to sound nutrition.

Do not overeat, however; keep your diet simple. Don't fill up on pizza, hot dogs and sodas and think that you have had a nourishing meal. These foods may provide energy, but there is no substitute for wholesome body-building foods.

Get into the habit of eating a good breakfast. Have fresh fruit or fruit juice, eggs, cereal, milk or cocoa and toast or a roll. A breakfast that consists of these foods will give you a good start for the day.

Enough sleep is the second requirement for good health. If you want to be in good physical condition, you must give your body a chance to revitalize itself, which is what it does when you are asleep.

If you are 12 years old, you should get about 10 hours' sleep each night. If you are in high school or in college, you need from 8 to 10 hours of nightly rest. On a long bike trip you should get from 10 to 12 hours' sleep. Sleep with a window open so you will have enough clean fresh air. It will help you sleep more soundly too.

Cleanliness is also important for physical fitness. Daily baths and showers help stimulate your blood circulation as well as keep your body clean.

You must exercise to get into shape for your bike tour. Select exercises that will develop the muscles you will be using as you cycle. A very good one is the bicycle exercise. Lie down on your back. Raise the lower part of your body so that your buttocks and legs are in the air, your arms bent at the elbows. Rest your hands at your waistline so that your arms support your body. Now, bend your knees and move your

Before beginning your trip to an unfamiliar area, consult a map of the route you will travel.

legs as if you were pedaling a bike. Continue this motion as long as you can. The first day, try for 25 times. Each day increase the number of cycles.

Here is a good exercise to strengthen your arms and shoulders. Extend your arms as if you were holding the handle bars of your bike. First slowly draw your arms to each side until they are extended outward from the shoulder. Then bring them forward again. Continue doing this until they begin to ache slightly. You will find you can do this exercise for increasingly longer periods each day.

Develop good posture. For proper cycling you need strong lung power, and if you don't give your lungs room to expand, you will not breathe properly. Stand straight, and learn to breathe fully, so that your lungs completely fill up with air. You will find that proper breathing makes a great difference in your endurance as a cyclist.

As soon as your body is in good physical condition, you will be able to tackle that long bike tour without worrying about exhaustion. Touring will become an invigorating sport, never an arduous chore.

HOW TO PACK AND GET YOUR BIKE READY FOR TOURING

It's best to use saddlebags that fit over your crossbar or rear wheel carrier. Or you can wrap your pack in a nylon, oilcloth or waterproof cover, and tie it to your metal carrier. Some riders carry their packs on their backs, but we have found this uncomfortable and unsafe. Metal carriers, wicker or metal baskets have limited capacities, whereas saddlebags are roomier. Fast riders don't like baskets or other carriers on the front of their bike, because they offer wind resistance and slow down touring speed.

It isn't your bike that will be carrying the load. It will be you! So spare yourself as much weight as possible. Thirty pounds is the accepted maximum weight to carry on a touring bicycle. Divide things among your group so that the weight will be equally distributed. And in packing your individual load, make it as compact as possible. Rolling kegs of oil in the hold of a ship can cause it to capsize. Similarly, cans that roll and rattle in your pack can be very annoying and may throw you off balance. So wrap cans securely in a woolen shirt or some heavy article of clothing.

Remember to take your tool kit and a tire-repair kit. For longer trips during which you may be far from a garage you should take along an extra inner tube and a hand pump. If you ride at night, include a flashlight and a few extra batteries. Of course, you will always take a first-aid kit on any tour or camping trip.

Before setting out, see that your bike is in good condition. Inspect it a few days before the trip, so that if it needs any complicated work, you can consult your local bike shop. Check the brakes; oil the movable parts; inflate the tires to the proper pressure, tighten all loose nuts and bolts.

Now, you're ready to select your clothing.

A group of hostelers view the St. Lawrence River from the historic Plains of Abraham in Quebec City.

WHAT CLOTHING WILL YOU NEED FOR TOURING OR BIKE CAMPING?

When touring or camping, you are "roughing it." Don't wear your best or newest sports clothes, but select clothing that is durable, comfortable, clean and light in weight.

Lightweight windbreakers are good for cool days, long sleeved cotton shirts for warmer ones. It is better to wear two lightweight shirts than a single heavy one, because you can remove one of them if the day becomes hot. T-shirts are practical because of their washability for both male and female riders, as are all nylon garments. You will need several pairs of socks (preferably wool), changes of underwear, sunglasses, a poncho or raincoat, a first-aid kit, a toothbrush, tooth paste or powder, a towel, soap and cleansing tissues.

For cycling through the woods, wear long trousers or slacks to keep your legs from getting scratched or infected by poisonous weeds. Denim and other hard-finish materials are excellent for outdoor wear. On cooler days wear ski pants (which fit the legs tightly and are tucked into the shoes) or dungarees over a pair of winter underwear. Sweaters aren't good for camping because they are easily snagged on bushes and become heavy and soggy when wet.

Woolen socks and waterproof shoes are excellent for hiking. But for biking and lounging around camp, you will want lighter shoes, perhaps moccasins. Wear leather work gloves while you do heavy work around camp; they are also good for cycling. Also, wear some kind of head covering in camp. Either a hunter's visor cap or a ski cap will protect your head from sun and from insects dropping off the trees.

It is both uncomfortable and extremely dangerous to have a scarf blowing in front of your face while cycling. A cap that is constantly on the verge of flying off your head is a great source of annoyance, too.

When choosing your bike wardrobe, be practical. Comfort and safety should be your first considerations.

WHAT IS A GOOD DIET FOR TOURING OR CAMPING?

Before you start out, eat a hearty breakfast of juice, eggs, bacon or ham and hot chocolate or milk. When biking, it is more important than usual to eat nourishing, well-balanced meals. You need to maintain your maximum energy. Stay away from such foods as hot dogs and soft drinks, which are not very nourishing, from thirst-producing things such as peanut butter and all highly seasoned items and from heavy foods (pancakes, for example). Eat large quantities of fresh fruits and vegetables and milk.

Plan to eat fairly often during the trip. It is better to eat many small meals or to "snack" than to have three large meals. When you stop for your hourly rest break, eat a piece of fruit or some chocolate. Oranges, tomatoes, grapes, pomegranates, peaches and plums are good thirst quenchers. Excellent sources of quick energy are: bananas, wedges of cheese, dried prunes or apricots, chocolate and hard-boiled eggs. It's smart to carry small cans of fruit or vegetable juice—the kind that does not have to be diluted. If you freeze these the night before you start, they will still be cold enough by the middle of the day to make a refreshing drink.

If you plan to cook out-of-doors or at a youth hostel, pack some cooking equipment. An all-purpose scouting knife complete with a can opener is a "must." It's smart to wrap snacks and sandwiches in aluminum foil, for you can use the paper later as a frying pan. Of course, you will avoid packing foods that are bulky, heavy or easily spoiled, for example fish.

When you are bike camping, carry nothing but staple foods. Buy meats, fish, milk, fruits and vegetables daily at the store nearest your camp. So unless you are camping in an area far from any shopping center, don't try to take enough food for an entire trip. Not only will you get fresher foods if you buy as you go, you will also have an opportunity to talk to people in the community. They will be able to answer important questions regarding terrain, road conditions, scenic and historic spots.

HOW TO STORE FOOD WHILE CAMPING

You'll have to find a good place to store food at camp. Even in bags, food kept on the ground will attract insects and small, hungry animals. Strange as it seems, the safest and cleanest method is to hang your food from a tree. Put your provisions in a sturdy bag (a pillowcase is good) and hang it from the limb of a tree. Here it will be shaded and relatively safe from animals.

Bottles and cans will stay cool in a stream or brook.

DOWNHILL AND MOUNTAIN BIKING

If you have ever ridden downhill for any distance at a great speed, you know how exciting it is. The experience is like flying. It's a wonderful free feeling, but you must be cautious or you may find yourself in trouble. Wind resistance becomes far greater—controls in stopping and steering become more difficult to apply.

Since most accidents seem to happen to tired riders, be sure you rest before taking a long drop or winding around a mountain. Be sure, too, that your bike is in top shape. Tighten all nuts, and tie down all gear. Stay at least 10 bicycle-lengths away from the cyclist ahead of you. If there's a motor vehicle ahead of you, stay at least 300 feet away to allow for quick stops and sudden turns.

This is the wrong way to ride down a steep hill. Always stay at least 10 bike-lengths away from the rider in front of you, keep on the right side of the road, and ride in a crouched position to lessen wind resistance.

Apply and release your brakes in a steady rhythm so that they won't wear out. There is another reason for this precaution; if you apply your brakes suddenly, you may be thrown over the handle bars. Watch for stones in the road. Slow down before every curve to be sure you can negotiate it at a certain speed. Once you are able to see around the curve, at the same time controlling your speed properly, you can release your brakes.

In descending rapidly it is wise to maintain a crouched position so as to minimize wind resistance and lower your center of gravity.

HEALTH PRECAUTIONS WHILE CYCLING

The most important rule is always to carry a first-aid kit. Even if you have never used it on previous trips and are tempted to leave it at home, *don't do it*. The one item you should never forget to pack is your first-aid kit.

You should also be familiar with first-aid procedures. It is a good idea to take a Red Cross first-aid course, and to carry the Red Cross first-aid textbook on all your trips.

It is essential that you learn to identify poisonous plants.

How often have you heard this warning: "Beware of those three-leaved plants—poison ivy" ? Observe it. These vines are real joy-killers. But poison ivy isn't the only plant to avoid. Poison oak and a little tree called poison sumac are equally dangerous.

The ivy has three shiny green leaves. Sometimes it grows as a bush; sometimes as a vine, twining itself around a tree, log or fence. In winter it has white berries and holds on to trees with its small, curly tendrils.

Poison sumac resembles other sumac trees except that it has white berries instead of the usual red ones. It grows in wet, marshy areas. Poison oak is not a tree, as its name suggests, but a vine. Its leaves look

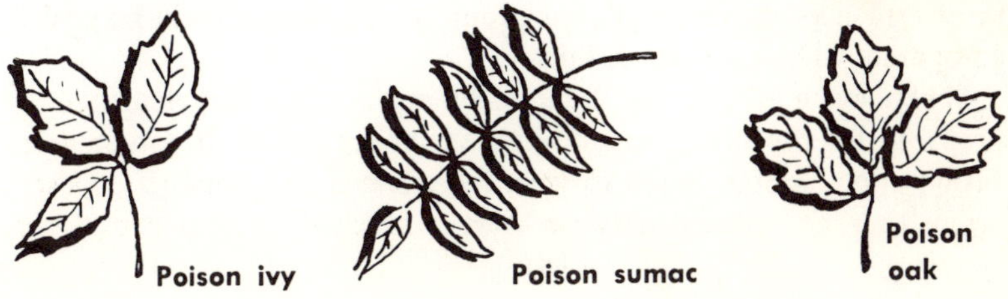

very much like oak leaves, but unlike those of the tree, the leaves of the vine can make you extremely uncomfortable if you touch them.

While walking or cycling through woods or along trails, keep your legs covered. If you think you have gone through a thicket of infectious plants, wash thoroughly with a strong laundry soap. Don't rinse off all the soap; let some of it dry on your body. It is wise to do this even if you are not sure you have touched a poisonous plant. The oils of these plants are so strong that they can get on your clothing; just by touching your own clothes, you may become infected. So keep that laundry soap handy!

Most snake bites are not particularly serious because most snakes are not poisonous. Nevertheless, you should send someone for a doctor to examine any snake bite; even if it isn't poisonous, it may be infected. Keep the victim quiet and warm. If you are quite sure the snake was of a poisonous variety (a rattler, coral snake, cottonmouth moccasin or copperhead) and you cannot get a doctor immediately, make a tight bandage and apply it two inches above the fang marks, between the bite and the injured person's heart. Next, cut two "x" marks $\frac{1}{4}$ inch deep and $\frac{1}{2}$ inch long right into the fang marks. Keep the wound open by suction. Suck out the poison, spitting it out and rinsing your mouth. Loosen the bandage for a little while every 30 minutes, and then tighten it again.

You may want to carry a snake bite kit which includes a suction bulb. Many cyclists, particularly in the Rocky Mountain area, always take such kits along. Fortunately, however, very few campers are bitten by snakes. Remember, snakes are just as afraid of people as we are of them. In most cases, they will go away.

If you burn yourself while working around the fire, apply some of the burn ointment from your first-aid kit. If the burn appears serious, go to the nearest doctor or hospital for proper treatment. Never neglect any serious injury, even if getting to a doctor disrupts your trip and inconveniences members of your group. Good campers will be glad to co-operate when someone is hurt.

When cycling, you are completely exposed to the elements. Be prepared for the strong sun. Sunglasses are essential. If you sunburn easily, apply suntan lotion to your face, hands and arms (if exposed) *before* they get burned. Always wear a kerchief or thin cotton cap, preferably one with a visor. You must shade your eyes and nose. The nose in particular is extremely sensitive to strong sun.

A head covering will also protect you from sunstroke. If you have a throbbing headache, a rapid pulse and a dizzy feeling, get into a cool, shady place at once. Lie down and put cold, wet compresses on your head and on the nape of your neck. If you feel very sick, send someone for the nearest physician.

Heat exhaustion is as dangerous as sunstroke. This is why you should always plan to rest during the midday hours of a hot, sunny day. It's a foolish cyclist who continues riding when he has these symptoms: weakness; pale and clammy skin; a slow pulse. These result when body salts are lost through excessive perspiration. You can prevent heat exhaustion by drinking water frequently and by taking salt tablets, or plain table salt, when you perspire excessively. If you feel you are being overcome by the heat, get into the shade, lie flat on your back and take some salt. If you don't feel better after a while, go to the nearest hostel or arrange to return home by train or bus.

When you pedal for a very long time, you may develop cramps in your legs or arms. Straighten out the affected limb and get off your bike. Massage the aching part to increase blood circulation. When you start cycling again, proceed slowly. Rest from time to time. When you reach your destination, take a hot bath or shower. This will ease your tired muscles.

Bike Camping

WHAT IS BIKE CAMPING?

Camping with a bike is a real challenge. It requires many skills—those of a camper and those of a cyclist combined. In the woods you are on your own, not only as a bike traveler following a daily route, but also as a camper making shelter and preparing food. Bike camping can provide many adventures. It leads you away from traffic, off the beaten path through the lovely unspoiled countryside where you can live close to nature for a while. With your bike you can enter remote areas off narrow byways and find delightful hidden spots for camping.

The main advantage in using your bike for camping is that you can explore the woods around your campsite and even go on fairly long side excursions. Woods and mountains offer endless fascinating experiences. Did you ever discover a tiny creek, follow it—and suddenly find that it had grown into a river? You will enjoy cycling around a lake shore, following intriguing trails and fording shallow streams.

On your bike you can cover much more ground (provided it's fairly level) than a hiker—and do it at much greater speeds. You can ride deep into the woods to study rocks, trees, flowers and birds at close range. If you go on bird hikes, take field glasses and a camera. A pocket-sized bird guide will give you the pleasure of being able to identify the birds you see. Guides to trees and wild flowers will also lend meaning to your nature hikes.

Your bike will come in handy in practical ways too. First, it will be easy to ride to the nearest stores for fresh provisions. You can use your bike as a tent prop and as a stepladder. With your bike as a pack horse, you will find it easy to load up your gear and move from one spot to another. Each time you break camp, the process will take less time. Soon you will be able to pack up and move on with great ease and very little loss of cycling time.

But let's not talk about breaking camp. Not yet!

If you're ready to go camping by bike, here's how to go about it.

WHERE SHOULD YOU CAMP?

First, decide where you want to camp. In travel books or magazines you may have seen colored photos of the high Sierras in California, of camping grounds in the Tennessee Valley area in North Carolina or of the North Woods of Minnesota. Perhaps the rolling hills of the Ozarks have a special appeal for you. Of course there are many national and state parks with camping facilities. They exist in almost all parts of the United States. If you settle on a campsite in a national or state park, find out whether you need a permit for camping; you may have to get permission from forest rangers or from the park commission. You can obtain pamphlets describing camping facilities in many state parks.

You may want to camp on land that is privately owned. Again, it is very important to obtain permission before you set up camp. Often, wild, uncultivated areas look like government property, but are actually owned by private companies or individuals.

Here are some additional tips. If you intend to hunt or fish, you'll need a license in most states. Generally, it makes sense to stick close to civilization, particularly if you are an inexperienced camper. Remain near towns and do not go deep into forests or mountains.

As soon as you have decided where you're going and have obtained any permits necessary, you can select your camping equipment.

WHAT EQUIPMENT SHOULD YOU TAKE FOR BIKE CAMPING?

What you take along depends on your trip—its duration, distance, the location of your campsite, the number of persons going and other factors. If you camp high up in the mountains, you will need many blankets, a good sleeping bag and warm clothes, because the temperature drops sharply at night. If you camp in summer near a lake, you will want mosquito netting.

Remember, everything you take on the trip should be light in weight and absolutely necessary. If you are in doubt about whether you will need an item, it's usually better to leave it at home. Here is a plan which some campers use to determine which equipment is essential. After returning from your trip, sort your equipment into three piles. In one pile put the things you didn't use at all. In the second pile place all the items you used only once or twice, and in the third put all the equipment you used every day. Then, on your next trip, take only those items from the third pile, and perhaps a few from the second pile. There is one very important exception to this method—a first-aid kit. Even if it is seldom or never used, always take it along.

The equipment you will need for your bike is the same as for any touring trip: a tool kit; a tube patch outfit and an extra inner tube. In addition, take along a waterproof cover to protect your bike from dew and rain.

Here is a list of standard camping equipment and supplies:

Sleeping bag (for a cycling trip get one that weighs about 6 pounds—either kapok-filled or lined with detachable layers of woolen material)
Blankets (if you do not have a sleeping bag)
Pup tent—for shelter
Scout knife
Hunting knife with sheath for protection
Small ax with covering over edge
Cooking kit (frying pan, saucepan, tin cup, knife, fork and spoon)
Food bag (an old pillowcase will do)
Match box (waterproof)
Compass
Canteen

First-aid kit
Flashlight (and extra batteries)
Field glasses and camera (not essential but they help make trip more enjoyable)
Maps (road and topographical)
Toilet paper
Soap (face soap and laundry soap for washing and poison ivy precaution)
Towels
Bicycle tool kit and pump
Knapsack
Bicycle saddlebag

A group of hostelers, their belongings safely — and comfortably — stowed away in saddlebags approach their destination, the city of Quebec in Canada.

SLEEPING BAGS

Sleeping bags combine the comforts of a warm blanket and a cozy bed in one light, compact roll. That's why they are so popular with campers, especially cyclists. The average sleeping bag weighs from $5\frac{1}{2}$ to 6 pounds, and there are about 100 varieties. Most of them are waterproof and these bags are filled with kapok, feathers or blanket material. They will keep you warm in weather as cold as 25° Fahrenheit. Specially-built and rather expensive down-filled bags for use in Arctic regions are comfortable in temperatures as low as 40° below zero. These bags weigh only $2\frac{1}{2}$ pounds. However, most of the standard bags on the market are warm enough for the average camper. Some bags, usually those made with blankets, are put together in layers so that on warmer nights you can zip out unnecessary covers.

When rolled up, your sleeping bag should not measure more than 6″ in diameter, 14″–16″ in width. Most people prefer mummy-shaped bags to rectangular ones. The "mummy" adherents say these bags are more draft-proof and fit more snugly than the others.

To carry your bag, roll it up and place it on the rear carrier of your bike. Bags are easier to handle than tents. For example, in the morning you can air your bag, roll it up—and leave it almost anywhere.

Use a waterproof ground cloth to keep the bag dry. Place the cloth on dry ground beneath the sleeping bag. The ground cloth can double as a waterproof cover for the sleeping bag while you are cycling, and you can also use it for a raincape or a picnic tablecloth. The best type of ground cloth is nylon.

How to Make Your Own Sleeping Bag

Good sleeping bags are expensive, so you may want to make your own. Take an old down comforter and fold it in half the long way; it will measure about 33″ × 84″. Sew up the bottom and then stitch halfway up the side opposite the folded edge. Now, attach "gripper" snaps to the unsewn upper half.

Presto! You've got yourself a sleeping bag as warm and light as many you can buy. Of course, it won't be waterproof, but waterproof sleeping bags have a disadvantage in that they don't "breathe." Moisture from your body condenses and remains inside a waterproof bag, making it cold and damp.

Here's how to make a sleeping sack to insert inside the bag:

1. Obtain an old single-sized sheet or two lengths of unbleached muslin.

2. Plan the sack to measure about 30″ × 78″.

3. Bring down a 24-inch flap from the top part of the sheet to fold over the top of the bag. This will keep the area around your face clean.

4. A gusset at each side of the sack will give you roominess.

5. Place your comforter over the sack.

There you are—a lined sleeping bag!

TENTS

Sleeping bags are more popular than tents. Since carrying space is limited on your cycle, a sleeping bag generally will fill the bill for short trips. But tents are still valuable. On longer camping trips away from shelters, a small pup tent will give you important protection from rain and unfavorable weather. A steady downpour can destroy your provisions and also make you very uncomfortable if you have no tent.

The best type for cyclists is the pup or mountain tent. The nylon variety is light, dries fast and folds down easily. It provides shelter for one or two people, weighs about 4 pounds, and costs about $10. This tent has collapsible upright aluminum poles. The entire tent folds down into a neat bundle 1′ × 2′, so it fits nicely into a saddlebag or on a carrier.

When you pitch your tent, set it so that the open side faces the most sheltered spot around you, usually south or east. This will permit sunlight to pour inside and will protect the tent from storms and strong winds, which usually come from the north or west.

After you have set it up, you will have to "ditch" your tent. Dig a ditch about 4 inches deep and 4 inches wide all around the tent. If it rains, this ditch acts as a gutter and keeps the rain from flooding the tent.

Remember not to touch the tent while you are inside it on a rainy day; water will leak through at the spot you touched. But if you accidentally bump against it, just press your finger against the spot you touched and draw it straight down along the side of the tent to the ground. The water will then flow off.

HOW TO CHOOSE A CAMPSITE

Of course, you will want a beautiful campsite, but in the final analysis, comfort and safety are more important. Although the view from a mountaintop may be awe-inspiring, a high, exposed campsite may get extremely windy at night. During the day it may be cool near a lake, but at night the mosquitoes will make you forget the loveliness of the lake.

Shady spots and hollows in dense forests are usually damp, making them favorite hangouts for insects. A heap of stones may shelter a litter of snakes. Stately oak trees may have gnarled roots that will dig into your back while you are trying to sleep. Don't camp too near a creek. A rainstorm miles away can cause the creek to swell and flood your campsite. Above all, watch out for poison ivy!

This list of "bewares" is not intended to frighten you. But you must avoid these dangers if you want your trip to be safe as well as fun. Comfort and safety come first. Select a campsite on high, open ground. If the land slopes to the south, you will have maximum sunshine and your tent will be dry. Also, see that your tent is near a water supply and as close as possible to the wood you will be using as fuel.

HOW TO BUILD A FIRE AND COOKOUT AREA

Fire will be your most useful servant: it will cook your food, keep you warm at night, and provide a cozy atmosphere.

Before setting up camp, decide where you want your fire. It should be far enough away from the tent and bikes for safety, yet not so far that it is inconvenient. Clear a six-foot circle of all grass, shrubbery and foliage that might burn, spreading the fire. After you have torn all these out, you are ready to build your fire.

A handy supply of wood can often save a dying fire. Don't put yourself in the position of having to yell for wood while you are trying to nurse a few tiny flames under a pot of soup. Always have different types of fuel near at hand. First, you will need tender twigs, dry leaves, paper and shavings for tinder. Then you should have a pile of kindling wood consisting of sturdier branches. Also have a pile of logs for firewood. Never cut growing trees; always use dead ones. You will find

Their tents providing shelter from the wind, bike campers gather round their campfire for some songs and laughter before turning in for the night.

that seasoned wood catches fire faster and burns better than fresh-cut green wood.

For a long-lasting fire, hardwood is best because it burns slowly and produces good embers. Hardwoods include hickory, beech, white ash, white or yellow birch, oak and sugar maple.

Softwoods are good for producing quick flames and for starting fires. You'll find softwoods like cedar and pine especially good for kindling. Experienced campers recommend using green wood for the back and side logs. This will keep the fire from spreading in diameter.

If it looks like rain, cover your wood with a waterproof tarpaulin, or bring a good supply of wood into your tent. Even if the rain catches you by surprise, you can usually find fairly dry wood under fallen trees. You may even be able to split a softwood log with your ax and scoop out the inner portions. Always dry out wet logs in the sun or near the fire.

You can build many types of fires. The hunter's fire is an easy-to-make cooking fire. Get two small green logs about five inches in diameter and lay them parallel, at right angles to the wind. Set the logs apart at a distance slightly less than the size of the cooking utensil that will rest on them. Now, build your fire between them. Use green side logs if you want this fireplace to last over a period of several days. Green logs, you will remember, don't burn as easily as seasoned ones.

If you don't have enough logs for a fireplace, make a trench fire. With a sharp stone dig a narrow trench about eight to ten inches deep and as long as your logs. Make it deeper at the end facing the wind. The fire burns from the deep end and you can shove in wood from the top. Set the utensils over the trench. A trench fire is sometimes better than the hunter type because it is underground and therefore protected from strong winds. A modification of the trench type is to use as a base a simple hole in the ground. This saves digging time.

To build a large reflector for any type of fire use a big stone or a fireproof structure as a back wall.

If you are inventive, you can construct cranes and other means of supporting pots over the fire. Always remember that your pot handle is probably hot. Save yourself burnt fingers by being careful. If you have difficulty reaching the pots, your fire is too large.

Never go away and leave a fire—not even for a few minutes. A sudden gust of wind can spread the fire and turn a growing forest into a wasteland. Always be near your fire, watching it.

Burning the garbage should be your last act before putting out the fire. Be sure the fire is really out when you leave. Pour water over it; then stamp it out. If you have large smoldering logs, throw them into a nearby lake, or pour water over them until you are sure they will not start burning again. Cover your campfire with dirt, sand or gravel after you have drenched it with water.

Fire is a helpful servant—but a destructive master.

HOW TO PURIFY WATER

If you bike camp near farms or in regular camping areas, you will have no trouble getting fresh, pure water. Since water is needed for drinking, cooking and washing, you must have an easily reached supply. The nearer it is to your campsite, the better. Contrary to popular belief, water in a flowing stream may be as unsafe as water from a still

Sometimes unpaved uphill roads are shortcuts worth taking on a bike trip.

pond. A flowing stream may carry down water from a contaminated source many miles away. Water found near a community is also likely to be contaminated. In a wilderness, chances are the water is relatively clean.

Boil all stream or river water for about 15 minutes before you drink it. Then allow it to cool. Toss it back and forth from one container to another. This process eliminates the flat taste which boiling gives the water. Water can also be purified by using Halazone, a chemical tablet sold at most drugstores.

To "clear" water you will need a water purifier which sells for about $8 at most camp supply stores. This is small and portable enough to carry on your bike. However, to be on the safe side, Halazone tablets should be used along with the purifier in case there are bacteria present. This method may appear cumbersome, but if you are away from civilization, you will have to accept certain inconveniences. After using chemicals in water, let it stand for an hour to get rid of the chemical taste.

Remember always to carry an ample water supply in your canteen when you are away from your campsite.

HOW TO MAKE A SHELTER WITH A BIKE

By now you have some idea of the immense usefulness of a bike. But do you know it can be used to make a shelter? This is how you do it. Tie your bike securely to a tree or to some other strong and stable object. Now, attach one end of a tarpaulin or similar covering to the handle bars of the bike. There's your shelter! It's that easy!

A covered bike can also be used as a windbreak. However, if you intend to use your bike for riding while at camp, don't get it rigged up for other purposes. Taking down and rebuilding your shelter or windbreak will become a nuisance.

HOW TO CARE FOR YOUR BIKE WHILE CAMPING

You will want to take good care of your bike, especially at night because heavy dew tends to rust metal parts. If it rains or there is an unusually heavy fall of dew, carefully wipe your bike with a dry rag. Always make sure that sharp stones, rocks and twigs are not pressing against your tires or spokes. Keep your bike standing or leaning at least 15 feet away from the sleeping or cooking area; this precaution will prevent the bike from injuring anyone in case it is toppled over by a strong wind.

HOW TO KEEP FROM GETTING LOST IN THE WOODS

If you leave highways and roads and decide to bike through the woods, you will have to be very careful. Learn to know the area where you are biking. As long as your bike leaves tracks, your chances of getting lost are very slight. You can follow your own tracks back to the highway or campsite. The time for real caution is when you leave your bike to explore the woods on foot. For one thing, you must remember exactly where you left your cycle.

It's a good idea to draw a simple map showing groves of trees, clearings, streams, hills, large rocks and lakes. Indicate the trails you will take. Mark off the spot where you set up headquarters for camping, resting or meeting other members of the group. With the help of your compass, mark off directions. Give each member of the group a copy of the map as well as a stick of chalk, a pencil, some small slips of paper, a few tacks, some safety matches and a compass. These items will be invaluable if anyone in your group gets lost.

If you bike in an area that is unfamiliar to you, you will have no map the first time you cover it. Here is another method of getting back to your meeting place without confusion or delay. As you ride along, make a chalk mark on the side of every fifth tree you pass. Your companions can also follow these marks, either to catch up with you or to explore the trail themselves.

If you decide to leave the path and veer off in an unmarked direction, scratch an arrow on a tree, rock or stump, or make one on the ground out of stones. If you don't have chalk, tack note paper to various trees. It is unwise to wander off the trail or path unless you are quite sure you can find your way back again.

Watch the sun for directions. For example, if the sun is setting, you can determine the direction of west. Then, when facing west, you will be able to ascertain the other directions. North will be to your right, south to your left, and east will be behind you.

WHAT TO DO IF YOU THINK YOU ARE LOST

1. Don't get panicky. Relax, but concentrate on remembering how you traveled. Try the method Boy Scouts use. Mark a tree on four sides so you can see the mark clearly from any direction. Then walk straight out from the tree for about 75 feet, moving in a circle with the marked tree in the center. As you go around, study the trees, the ground and the surrounding area for familiar signs.

2. Leave a note for your friends telling the direction in which you are heading. Tack it to a tree, write it on a rock or spell it out on the ground with small stones.

3. Try to find a stream. Then follow it downstream. Streams flow into larger bodies of water, and eventually they will lead you to towns and people.

4. Look for high ground. You can see farther from a hill, mound, large rock, or tall tree. Climb up and try to see a familiar landmark—a road, a valley or a clump of trees that looks familiar. Try to call out from this high spot. Your voice will carry fairly well from high ground.

5. Follow such signs of civilization as telephone poles, power lines, cleared trails, sounds of trains or autos. These should lead you out of the woods.

6. Send up a smoke signal. Clear a large area of grass and brush and build three fires of semi-green wood, grass and mossy fern. Build them far enough apart so that they will send up three separate smoke columns. Someone will see them and come to your rescue. If it is cold, of course the fire will warm you.

7. If it is getting dark, stay where you are. Try to make yourself as comfortable as possible. Look for a dry shelter on high ground. Get behind a large rock or tree that will act as a windbreak.

Above all, don't lose your head. The clearer your thinking in any emergency, the better you will handle it.

How to Ride a Bike

So far we've assumed that everyone knows how to ride a bike. It's so much fun that everyone *should* know how. But maybe you've just been planning to learn. If that's the case with you, don't put it off any longer. The sooner you master cycling, the sooner you'll be able to participate in the races and games, the tours and camping expeditions we've already described.

Beginners should not be afraid. The simple instructions beginning below will get you off to an excellent start. Or maybe you're an intermediate cyclist—pretty good but not yet skilled enough for long trips. In that case, you will want to read pages 85-86.

Even expert cyclists may pick up some tips from the following pages.

IF YOU'RE A BEGINNER . . .

Ask any cyclist—he will tell you that riding a bike is the easiest thing in the world. "Just hop on and ride away. That's all there is to it!"

It *is* easy to ride a bike, but it's not that easy, especially if you're a beginner. As a learner you will have to overcome certain fears: first, the fear of falling off and getting hurt; second and perhaps more important, the fear of injuring your dignity. Both are natural fears.

Of course, you can't learn to ride just by sitting down and reading these pages. But you will find suggestions here that will help make riding easier for you. The only way to learn is by doing. Take your bike by the handle bars, gather up your confidence and you are ready to begin.

You can teach yourself either by the "trial and error" method, or you can have a friend help you. Having an understanding friend assist is the easier and the more common method. However, be sure the friend you select has a thorough understanding of the fundamentals of riding, so that he can demonstrate how it is done and help you in balancing, turning, stopping, mounting and dismounting.

Take your "teacher" and your bike to a wide street or yard where there is no traffic. An area with a slight declining slope is best, as it will give you an automatic starting push. Adjust your bike saddle so that as you sit on it, your feet are flat on the ground. This will lower your center of gravity, enabling you to balance easily. If you know that you can stop simply by putting your feet on the ground, you will feel quite secure.

Before you get on, study the bike and notice the way it balances. Roll it back and forth. Notice that if you tilt it toward the right, you will be able to keep the bike from falling by turning the handle bars to the right. Tilt it to the left; then turn the handle bars to the left, and balance will be immediately restored. This is the first important principle for you to remember. So, if you are riding slowly and your cycle begins to fall to one side, turn the handle bars very slightly in that direction and you will keep your balance.

The next step is to get on the bike. Have your friend hold it and push it slowly until you begin to get the "feel." Try out the pedals and brakes to see if you can balance the bike while your friend is still holding on to it.

As your helper walks along pushing the cycle, try to keep your head up. Don't let your eyes become glued to your feet or to the wheels. Look straight ahead and try to get accustomed to the sensation of riding. If your feet happen to slip off the pedals, don't look down at them; you may lose your balance. Just stay calm. Your feet will find their way back to the pedals again.

When you have enough confidence, ask your friend to let go and try to keep the bike moving all by yourself. A slow-moving bike is likely to tip, so pedal quickly. Even if you forget these instructions and fall, don't be afraid. Very few people get badly hurt while learning to ride.

Brakes operate easily. With coaster brakes, all you do to stop is push the top pedal backward. Use a slight pressure. You will stop too suddenly if you *jam* your foot back on the pedal. You operate rim brakes by pulling

When the pedal is at "six o'clock" your leg should be almost straight.

up on the hand levers. Now, as the bike slows down, put your foot out and "catch" the ground again.

Perhaps by now you have enough courage to start out by yourself. To begin, place the right pedal higher than the left. (Of course, if you are a "lefty," you will probably start with the left pedal.) In any case, straddle the bike and put one foot on the pedal that is higher and slightly ahead of the other one. As you press down on that pedal, give yourself a push with the foot that is on the ground, raise it to the other pedal, and presto! You are riding. Both the push-off and pressing down on the pedal should be done at the same time. You will get the rhythm of it after a little practice.

To pedal your bike correctly, put the ball of your foot on the pedal, flex your knee and sit with your body relaxed and forward.

George Bernard Shaw, famous playwright, critic and veteran cyclist, had this advice to give: "To learn biking, try to stand a penny on its edge. Impossible when the penny is stationary, easy when it is rolling. Once convinced of this, rush the machine and jump on."

When you start moving, keep pedaling. Remember that you have brakes. You can stop any time, but don't try to stop with your foot if the bike is going too fast. In dismounting it is safer to get off from the right side, away from traffic.

Many beginners feel confident of their riding ability until they try to turn. At this stage you may become anxious if the bike leans to one side and threatens to topple over. A good way to keep your balance when turning is to put out your leg in the direction of the turn. Then if you feel the bike leaning over too much, put your toe on the ground and use it as a pivot. As soon as you retain your balance and direction, put your foot back on the pedal.

Don't lean all your weight on the handle bars as many beginners do. Keep your weight evenly distributed between the pedals and the saddle. This is the correct position for ease and speed, and it will give you maximum control over your bike.

Learning to ride is just like learning any new skill. Some people find it easy; others difficult. It may take you three lessons to learn, or it may take less than an hour. For some adults, mastering a bike may take as many as fifteen lessons. Those who do have trouble should not be "shoved" into learning how to ride.

But most people, especially youngsters, have no beginning difficulty. You will learn at your own pace, individually. Whatever initial problems you have, don't become discouraged. You do not have to be a professional to enjoy cycling.

IF YOU'RE AN INTERMEDIATE . . .

You are no longer a novice—so readjust your bike saddle. Raise it so that you can barely touch the ground with your toes. The handle bars should be the same height as the saddle, and the grips should not be so low that they will strain your hands and wrists. After fairly long trips, many beginning cyclists complain of stiffness or pain in their hands and wrists. You can avoid this if you have the saddle and handle bars at the proper height, in correct relationship to each other.

Don't sit rigid and straight. "Perfect posture" is not suitable for riding a bike. You should lean forward a bit from the hips, not from the shoulders. Relax! Don't lean over so far that you are all hunched up over the handle bars like a racer. This will result in a stiff back, for it is not the correct posture for normal riding.

Pedal evenly and exert equal pressure with each foot. Uneven pressure will cause you to wander and zigzag all over the road. Only the balls of your feet should touch the pedals, pressing as you push from the hips. Never pedal with your instep or heel.

In pedaling use your ankles and don't keep your feet stiff. The movement of each foot should come from the ankle as it first follows, and then pushes the pedal in a circular motion. This method, called "ankling," is very important if you want to become a good cyclist. Put your ankles to work so that they always exert steady pressure on the pedals, and so that your feet push the pedals in a circle. At first your ankles will tire quickly, so give them a rest from time to time. As your muscles get stronger, ankling will become natural to you. It will help you climb hills and will increase your pedaling efficiency. Try it. See the difference!

When you ride down a steep hill, use your brakes or your cycle may run away with you. Another thing to remember, especially while you are still increasing your proficiency, is not to mount your cycle on an upgrade. If you get off to a slow start, you may slide backward.

Until you feel completely competent on your bike, take as many short trips as possible. Extend their length as your muscles grow stronger and your experience increases. Before you know it, you'll be whizzing along, enjoying the countryside without a thought for the mechanics of riding.

Some cyclists wonder what to do about the dog problem. While slowly pedaling along, you may be suddenly surprised by the loud barking of a dog. A fierce-looking mastiff is running toward you. With teeth bared, he chases—and you hold your breath and wait for him to take a chunk out of your leg. But don't get nervous. Yell at the dog. If that doesn't drive him away, try to outdistance him. Very few cyclists get nipped by dogs. They only get to their destinations a little faster than they had expected.

RACING

You will need special training if you are interested in racing. You have to be an expert cyclist with a great deal of experience, and you will need a racer, built according to your own specifications. See pages 90-91.

Posture is different in racing than in ordinary riding; for racing your body should be well forward. The saddle is hard and high, and the handle bars are dropped low so that there is less wind resistance and more energy is generated.

Whether you race with friends or with a club, you will have to train to keep slim and strong, and to build up your wind and endurance. Training includes a special diet of non-fattening foods, sleeping on your back with the window wide open, and regular daily outdoor training periods on your racer. If you are a serious racer, you will have to have special racing shoes, goggles, gloves for braking, trunks, a crash helmet, and some type of exercising cycle in your house.

To be a racer you must train with the smallest possible amount of bike equipment. This will develop speed in your legs. Always train without cleats, straps or toe clips. Every trainee should ride at least 5 miles each day.

However, you should be careful not to *overtrain.* Many young racers wear themselves out. Cyclists under 16 years of age should not train too rigorously and should not ride more than 60 miles a day.

Remember, you do not have to have a deadly serious attitude toward racing to enjoy it. Every cyclist loves a good run on his bike, and you can enjoy the races described here whether you include them in a bike rodeo, race meet or simply run them off casually with a group of friends. As long as you compete with someone of almost similar ability, racing is always fun.

How to Select Your Bike

Perhaps you've been renting a bike, borrowing one from a friend or even using your older brother or sister's castoff. If so, you must be eager to get your own bicycle. There are several types of cycles and before you select one, you should understand the characteristics of the major types.

More middleweight and lightweight touring types are produced in the United States than in any other nation in the world. We also import bikes, mainly from England, Italy and France. Those imported are all touring models, the forerunners of the American lightweight. The imports sell for about the same or for slightly higher retail prices than American makes of similar quality and type.

The major differences in bikes are in weight and type of tire.

WHAT TYPE OF BIKE IS THE BEST FOR YOU?

Middleweight and Novelty

If you're a beginner, you are likely to want a middleweight bike. This is the favorite type for most youngsters because it's tough and can take plenty of wear and tear. Since most cyclists are young people, you will see the middleweight model most often. It has bouncy tires, a comfortable, springy seat and a low center of gravity. It absorbs road shocks and is not easily damaged by rough usage. If you think you may eventually want to motorize your bike, get this model; some manufacturers guarantee the middleweight frames for use with a motor.

The middleweight model weighs from 40 to 55 pounds and is useful for short trips. You can use it for touring, but you will tire much more quickly than on a lightweight model. The middleweight bike generally is equipped with foot brakes. Its main disadvantage is that gears can't be added, which means that you have to travel at the same gear ratio both uphill and down. Although some experienced cyclists sneer

There's a bike to attract every member of the family. While lightweights are popular with adults, many youngsters prefer middleweight or novelty models.

at the middleweight bike, calling it a "truck," its elaborate gadgets and motor styling make it the choice of many.

A novelty bike popular with the younger cyclists has large handlebars and an elongated seat called a banana seat. The 20-inch frame gives it a lower center of gravity, and the large handlebars help the rider make quick turns. Some riders learn to do tricks on these bikes. One stunt, for example, is to ride on the rear wheel with the front wheel raised—bronco style.

Lightweight

If you are interested in hosteling, touring or camping, you will want a lightweight wheel, especially if it is equipped with gears. Even if you only want to take short trips in the neighborhood, you may still prefer the touring model. This type is suitable for all-around use. Although it is slightly less durable than a balloon-tire bike, the lightweight combines speed with strength. Many an ardent cyclist owns both a lightweight and a racer. More and more adults are riding the lightweights, convinced of their traveling superiority.

Simply made, the lightweight is quiet, fast, graceful and comfortable. It weighs 25 to 40 pounds and has no tanks, only essential supports. The man's model has only a single crossbar. Saddle, fender and frame are light. To save weight, many models are made without chain guards or rear carriers. The better-quality frames are made of manganese molybdenum tubing, a material that is widely used in airplane construction because it combines lightness with strength.

A trend in the lightweight field is the use of dropped handle bars, as on racers. On all lightweights, handle bars and rims are chrome-plated and spokes are rust-resistant. Foot brakes can be attached to the lightweight, but the best models have rim type, hand-controlled brakes. British models generally come with more equipment than do American lightweights; usually they have a headlight, carrier and tool kit.

Besides lightness, the great advantage of this model is its variable gear shift. See page 99. You'll see! The gear shift will enable you to speed up hills and spurt ahead on a straightaway.

Racer

Only an expert cyclist should consider a racer. Speed is all-important, more so than durability. Many racers are custom-made, each built according to specifications which you as a veteran rider must furnish. Part by part—tires, wheels, saddle, pedals, frame, gear ratio, hubs, crank, handle bars and brakes (if any)—this bike is made to your order. Custom-produced racers naturally cost much more than factory-built types. However, some factory models have many preferred racing features and sell for less than $90.

The racer is used either on special tracks or on smooth roads. Bike games, camping and touring on bumpy and rutted roads may be too much of a strain for the racer's thin tires and light frame. In its severe simplicity, the racer possesses only the essential elements of the bicycle. Since speed is its objective, extra weight such as fenders, brakes and supporting rods are seldom placed on the bike. Racers weigh only 15 to 30 pounds. A strong lightweight metal, duralumin, is generally used for the frame. Since it has no brakes, the racer is unsafe in traffic. Riders usually wear gloves, and stop the bike by reaching over the handle bars and slapping the front tire.

The racer uses high-pressure tires which have to be kept well inflated. Its tire traction is probably no wider than a quarter of an inch. The glued-on type of tire has a sewn-in tube, and can withstand air pressures which could blow out most car tires. The wheels generally have wooden rims. Dropped handle bars make it possible for you easily to assume the racing position—body well forward and low to overcome wind resistance. Because of the racing position, the saddle doesn't perform the same function as on other models. It is a hard piece of leather to sit *against*, rather than on. Since the saddle is rigid, you will find it easy to direct your energy to the point of acceleration—the pedals.

With small, narrow, high-pressure tires, a firm saddle, and nothing to absorb bumps, the racer rides hard. However, it isn't unusual to hear racing cyclists who cover 75 to 100 miles a day talk about the comfort of their "steed." Getting used to a racer is a process you may not enjoy, but if you love the thrill of speed, it will pay off in excitement.

But before selecting any model, first consider for what purpose you are going to use your bike. Then, consider your ability and experience. There are so many cycles available, you'll have no trouble choosing exactly the right bike for you.

WHAT IS YOUR BIKE SIZE?

Bicycles are measured by wheel size and frame size. Wheel sizes run 20″, 24″, and 27″. The 27″ size is the standard adult and teen-age wheel. This includes lightweight and middleweight bikes. Equipped with adjustable handle bars and seat, it suits riders 5 feet or more in height. The 20″ and 24″ wheels are recommended for youngsters, and your dealer can fit the bike to a child's height.

If you take the average 27″ touring wheel size, you may also want to know the frame size. A 19″ frame will fit people under 5 feet tall. A 21″ frame will fit persons from 5 feet in height to 5 feet 9 inches; a 23″ frame is designed for cyclists from 5 feet 10 inches to 6 feet, and a 24″ frame is for those over 6 feet in height. You can determine the size of the frame by measuring the length of the frame tube that extends from the chain sprocket up to the saddle.

The saddle is at the right height when, with one leg straight and the pedal at "6 o'clock," your lower heel rests on the pedal. When, with the seat properly adjusted and your hands on the handle bar grips, you lean slightly forward and feel comfortable, the handle bars are in the correct position.

You can also check bike size by sitting on the saddle while the bike is in regular standing position with tires inflated. If you are just able to touch the floor with your toes, the frame size and saddle height are correct. If your feet rest flat on the floor and your legs are straight, the saddle is too low and should be raised.

Parts and Accessories

WHAT PARTS SHOULD YOU USE?

Essentially, a bicycle is simply a frame designed to hold a rider between two wheels of equal size so that he can move forward on the same physical principle as a rolling ball. You can ride on a frame and wheels only (as on a racer), but for more enjoyable traveling you will probably want to equip your bike with some of the new and useful parts and accessories.

Brakes

First, let's discuss the three kinds of brakes: coaster, rim or rod, and the internal-expanding hub brake.

The coaster is used on all middleweight bikes and on some lightweights. The body of the brake is in the back hub of the wheel and you operate it by back pedaling. It is free running, so if you apply light pressure, you will stop gradually. To stop suddenly, apply firm pressure.

The rim or rod type of brake operates directly on the rim of the wheel. Two slender wire arms (some bikes have rods or cables) drop from the handle bars, curving around corners and angles as necessary, to reach the rims of both front and back wheels. Rubber shoes or blocks are attached to the ends of the wire arms. When you apply the brake from the handle bars with your fingers, these shoes press against the rims of the wheels. A small coil spring exerts the tension which brings the brake back to its original position when you are not using it.

You can adjust these brakes by taking up or letting out the cables. Turn the nut and bolt on the cable in the direction which gives you the proper adjustment. You can adjust rods in the same way as cables—by lengthening or shortening them. Be sure you keep your wheel rims dry and clean at all times; otherwise, rim brakes will not grip firmly.

The third type of brake is the internal-expanding hub. Although coaster and rim brakes are safe and dependable, the hub brake is considered the most powerful. It is fully enclosed in the hub, attached to the handle bars by a cable running to the hub. When the cable is pulled up from the handle bars, a piece of steel forces the brake shoe to spread inside the drum. This mechanism is similar to the auto brake. Since it is enclosed, the hub brake is protected from rain, snow or dirt. This is its greatest advantage.

Lights

Battery-operated lights are the most widely used. Most deluxe balloon-tire bikes have battery headlights and taillights. Some riders prefer an ordinary flashlight clamped in a handle bar bracket because it can be taken out and used for other purposes in camping or touring. The disadvantage of the battery-operated light or flashlight is that it burns out when the battery is exhausted.

The generator type of light, which requires a set, is more expensive than the battery type, but requires hardly any upkeep. It gives more light than the battery type (the popular 12-volt generator supplies more light than six batteries), and neither the headlight nor the taillight

Attach strips of light-reflecting Scotchlite to your fenders—and clothing—for safe night-riding.

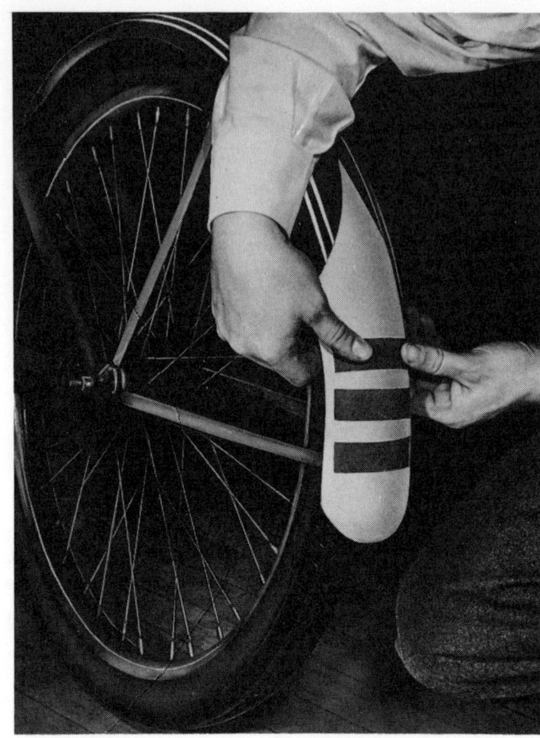

Strips of Scotchlite on the rear fenders will warn motorists and other cyclists of your presence on dark roads.

burns out as long as the bike is in motion. (The power fails though, when the cycle stops.) The generator unit is set against the tire and power is run directly from it. One type of generator is built into the front hub like a hub brake, and is similarly protected from dirt and rain.

Be sure to fasten red reflectors to the rear carrier or fender of your cycle. If you have a racer, place several small reflectors on the pedals or wear a reflector on the back of your belt. Wear a white sweater or shirt for night riding.

Scotchlite is a light-reflecting material consisting of thousands of tiny glass beads fixed to an adhesive plastic or fabric base. During the second World War it was used to mark invasion beaches, harbor and channel buoys, aircraft landing strips, paddles of pneumatic aircraft, lifeboats and traffic signs. More recently it has been adapted as a safety device for bicycles, automobiles, trains, buses and clothing. Like adhesive tape, the product comes in varying widths and is a good supplement to your regular lighting unit. However, it should not be used in place of a headlight or taillight.

Saddles

Saddles vary with the type of bike on which they are used. A balloon-tire bike saddle usually is made of top-grain leather, chrome springs, sponge-rubber padding and is fitted with a chrome guard at the back. It may be almost as soft and springy as a motorcycle seat.

Saddles on lighter bikes are generally lighter, harder and smaller. Although it is difficult to get used to a hard saddle, racers will tell you it pays off in the long run. A saddle that has no "give" will not waste your pedaling energy, as will a springier seat.

The racing saddle is simply a narrow piece of leather. The lightweight touring saddle may be equipped with a short coil spring and mattress padding, or it may be simply a wide piece of pliable leather. As with other equipment, you will have to test your saddle for comfort and for its suitability to your individual needs.

Handle Bars

All racers and advanced touring bikes come with dropped handle bars. The drop may be extreme (as on professional racers) or slight (for the novice tourist). Because of the drop, your body is pitched forward, eliminating much wind resistance and permitting very efficient pedaling. If you want to rest your arms, assume a more upright position and rest them on top at the middle of the bars.

Not all touring bikes have dropped handle bars. Many lightweight tourists have level or flat handle bars, or a drop of not more than a few inches. Some balloon-tire models are equipped with upturned or "steer horn" handle bars. The new models of good quality bikes, both light and heavyweight, now come equipped with chrome rustproof handle bars.

You will want to equip your handle bars with grips, either light rubber or leather, or simple ones made from heavy tape. Do not use spongy grips; they become hot and sticky.

Pedals

Most cycles come with rubber pedals. But racers and advanced touring bikes have the metal (or rat trap) type of pedal. These have an advantage over the rubber pedals, which are slippery in rain. The metal type also has teeth to give better gripping ability. If you have a choice, choose metal pedals.

Fenders

If you intend to ride in all kinds of weather, you will definitely need fenders to protect you from mud and dust. All middleweight bikes and most lightweights are manufactured with steel fenders, but racers are fenderless. Four materials are used in making fenders—steel, aluminum, celluloid and dural (an aluminum alloy). Steel is heavy and firm; aluminum, light and bendable; celluloid, light but prone to warping; dural, light and firm, is probably the best.

Tires

Middleweight tire inner tube dimensions are 26 × 1.75 inches. They inflate to about 35 pounds.

The lightweight tire measures 27 × 1¼ inches. Weighing 23 ounces and inflated with 50 to 70 pounds of air, they can endure heavy touring.

Track-racing tires, as light as 6 or 7 ounces and as narrow as ¾ of an inch wide, are inflated up to 150 pounds for use on the six-day bike race track. The inner tube is held in place by being sewn to the inside casing, thus making a completely sealed tube. Road-racing tires are 1 to 1⅛ inch wide, and are inflated to about 100 pounds.

WHAT ACCESSORIES SHOULD YOU USE?

Carriers and Saddlebags

There are almost as many types of carriers as there are styles of bikes. Many middleweight models come equipped with streamlined all-metal carriers to which your gear can be tied. Trim, light carriers of aluminum tubing, new on the market, are especially recommended for touring use. These can easily hold a sleeping bag. When you are not using them, they take up very little space.

If you use your bike for delivering or marketing, you will want to have a wire basket mounted on the handle bars. Wicker baskets are also fine for marketing and are used in hosteling and touring.

For long bike trips and for camping, use saddlebags. They serve as large double knapsacks—one on each side of the back wheel. You will

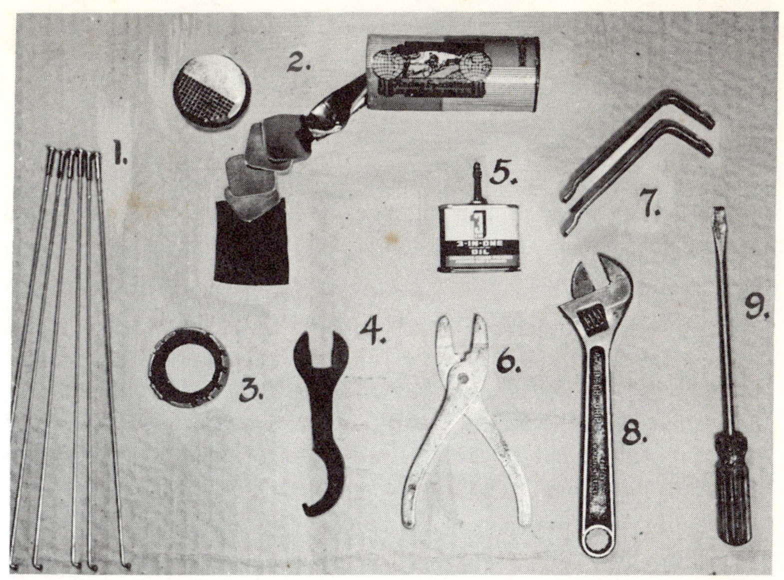

On any camping trip or tour you should take a tool kit to handle emergency repairs. A complete tool kit includes (1) extra spokes, (2) tire repair kit, (3) nipple or spoke wrench, (4) wrench, (5) oil can, (6) pliers, (7) tire irons, (8) adjustable wrench, and (9) screw driver.

have to get a back carrier in order to keep the saddlebags in place; do this by slipping a tape through the carrier. The carrier will support a tent or sleeping bag and you will probably find that the saddlebags will hold the rest of your gear. Saddlebags are also convenient for transporting provisions from stores to your hostel or campsite.

Bike Basket Cover

You can use the largest sized pliofilm refrigerator bowl cover as a suitable rainproof protector over a wicker basket. You can also make one from a piece of plastic material and strong elastic; shape it to fit snugly over the basket.

Locks

Some of the new deluxe heavyweight bikes are equipped with built-in fork locks. All you need is a key. If your bike does not have this lock, get a simple padlock or a long shank lock. You can lock the sprocket chain to two spokes, or lock the bike with a chain to a post.

Bells and Horns

To be safe you must have a sound-warning device on your bike. Bells are pleasant and probably more suitable for bicycles than the more commanding horns. Take your choice, but use something!

Cyclometers

Cyclometers are devices which compute distances covered. If you travel a great deal, this meter is a "must." You will find it a great help to know the number of miles you have traveled, and the amount you have still to go. It is best to fasten this instrument near the front hub, where it will be out of the way and inconspicuous. The counter is moved by a striking pin on a wheel spoke.

Toe Clips

The toe clip is a special gadget which increases pedaling energy when attached to the metal (rat trap) pedals of a lightweight or racer. It is a piece of steel made to curve around the upper part of your toe to form a steel pocket. As your foot revolves, extra power is generated. Be careful, however. If you take frequent spills, the toe clip can cause trouble; it tends to hold the foot to the pedal.

Pumps

Many English bikes come equipped with small, light air pumps. Made of plastic, these pumps are neatly attached to the frame bar. You operate them by hand and will find one particularly useful on trips which take you far from service stations. You can purchase such a pump as an accessory if your bike didn't come with one.

Directional Rear Light

Twin-arrow lights mounted on your rear light will indicate the direction in which you intend to turn. The light switch is located on the front frame of the bicycle. A reflector, set on the same mounting just below the directional arrows, serves as a taillight for the bicycle. Because it adds extra weight, you probably will not want to use a directional rear light on a racer or touring bike.

Tool Kit

Your tool kit should include tire repair equipment, a screw driver, a spoke wrench, an ordinary wrench and an oil can. If you are going on a long trip, take along a few extra spokes and tie them to the crossbar.

Radio

You can attach a small portable radio to your rear carrier and play it while you are riding. If you prefer, you can pack it for use after you have set up camp.

Rearview Mirror

This mirror, which is similar to a car mirror, is attached to the left side of the handle bars. It is a helpful safety aid, for you can see rear traffic approaching.

Safety Vest

This is a lightweight vest of brilliant "dayglo" orange. It is made of acetate rayon, can withstand rain and snow, and reflects the light.

Cyclo-pedia

A cycling handbook and catalogue of supplies and equipment, the cyclo-pedia contains valuable information on cycling. Published by Gene Portuesi (311 North Mitchell, Cadillac, Michigan, 49601), it sells for $1.00.

GEARS

Gearing is a method of gaining wheel power on a bike. For example, when riding uphill you should shift to a lower gear; otherwise, the sprocket revolutions will slow down and you will find yourself tending to "stand up," trying to develop enough power to climb the hill.

In the early days of bike riding the pedal was attached to the large front drive wheel, which was about 70 inches in diameter. There were no gears; the power was applied to the pedals in the same way as on a child's tricycle. The drive wheel made exactly as many revolutions as the foot of the rider.

Today you can exert power on the standard 27″ inch wheel, through the ratio of two sprockets and a chain, equal to the power of a wheel 70 inches in diameter. This increase in power is made possible by gear-

ing. In other words, the modern 27″inch wheel can be pedaled by means of gears at the same ratio as that of the antiquated high wheelers, and with much greater ease.

For pleasant riding you should have gears. Most lightweight touring bikes have three-speed, five-speed or ten-speed gears, which help to "level off hills" in one gear and, in another, give you good pedal pressure on level or downhill runs. Some gears have as many as fifteen speeds which can be adjusted to suit your cycling skill and the terrain you are negotiating. The greater the variation in terrain, the greater should be the variation in available gears.

High gear is for fast riding. The greater the difference between the number of teeth in the chain and the rear sprockets, the higher the gear. At the higher gear, your foot will make relatively few revolutions for the speed obtained. You will not tire quickly if you use high gear on a level or declining slope.

The smaller the difference between the number of teeth in the chain wheel and the rear sprockets, the lower the gear. At the lower gear, your foot will make more revolutions than in high, and the number will more closely approximate the number of revolutions made by the wheel. Low gear is best for hill climbing. In this gear your foot revolves quickly enough to give you the momentum necessary to accelerate uphill. Don't use low gear on level stretches or downhill; you will find your pedals revolving too quickly and you will rapidly become tired.

When going downhill or when developing speed on a level road, you should shift to high gear. This slows down the speed of sprocket revolutions. If you do not shift to high, your legs will be moving so fast you will not feel the pressure of the pedals against your feet.

On fairly level roads with a few easy hills, a three-speed gear should be adequate. However, if you are going through country which includes both mountains and level areas, you should consider getting a ten-speed gear.

For example, let's assume that 70 revolutions per minute is your normal pace on a level stretch. As you approach a hill, you will have to change gears to keep producing your normal, comfortable 70 revolutions. Although you could probably maintain 70 without changing gears, it would be such a strain that cycling would no longer be a pleasurable sport. With the gears, however, you can move smoothly along at the best cadence for you.

If you are riding over hills of varying steepness, you might want to use two lower gears. Again, this depends upon the terrain. Of course, on a bike with ten or twelve speeds you will be able to take all kinds of hills, but if the general direction of your trips leads you over fairly level country, you will be satisfied with only three speeds.

Select a bike whose gear ratio is the most comfortable for you. Try a number of bikes with different gear ratios before you decide on one. The most useful gears run from 60 to 80. Girls generally use the lower ones—50 to 70. These are the hill-climbing gears. Gears from 70 to 80 are best for level roads and downhill. Racers are geared from 80 to 90.

Find your own gear ratio by using this formula:

Number of teeth in your chain wheel sprocket..........................

Multiplied by the diameter of your wheel...............................

Divided by the number of teeth in your rear sprocket.................

Equals your gear.

Example:

Number of teeth in your chain wheel sprocket.......................... 48

Times the diameter of your wheel.. 27

1,296

Divided by the number of teeth in your rear sprocket................. 20

Equals your gear.. 64.16

In the example given above, the gear was 64 plus. This is a useful road-climbing gear.

The gears we have been discussing are fixed. If your bike has hand brakes and no foot brakes, you can attach gears with different speeds. With variable three-speed gears, you can adjust to a normal speed at 64, shift into a low of 49 to climb a steep hill, or shift into a high gear of 85 on a level stretch. For the most pleasurable touring you need different gearing for uphill and downhill travel. A three-speed gear can be fitted to any bike equipped with independent hand brakes. For the most part, this means lightweights. Variable gearing, years ago invented in England, has now become widely used in America, and has had much to do with the growing popularity of biking.

Bike Safety

Are you a "safety first" bike rider? Statistics put the responsibility for traffic accidents involving bikes squarely on the cyclist. Figures show that many bike accidents in the United States are caused by bikes in bad repair, and that many other accidents occur because the cyclist violates traffic rules.

CAUSES OF BIKE ACCIDENTS

1. Cyclist makes improper turn.
2. Cyclist fails to signal correctly.
3. Bike lacks proper controls (poor brakes, no head lamps, no rear reflectors, or rider fails to use them).
4. Carrying an extra rider.
5. Cyclist runs into open auto doors.
6. Excessive speed.
7. Cutting in between cars.
8. Hitching a ride.
9. Riding against traffic.
10. Not coming to full stop when riding down driveway to street.
11. Riding when cyclist doesn't feel well or is tired.
12. Carrying a person on the handle bars.
13. Making repairs on the road.
14. Not riding on correct side of road.
15. Riding in busy sections.

The following rules were drawn up by a group of bike safety experts. If you observe them at all times, you probably will never be involved in an accident.

BIKE SAFETY RULES

1. Observe all traffic regulations—red and green lights, one-way streets, stop signs.

2. Keep to the right and ride in single file. Keep a safe distance behind all vehicles.

3. Have a white light on the front and a danger signal on the rear for night driving. Wear white or light-colored clothing at night.

4. Have a satisfactory signaling device to warn of your approach. Always ride at a safe speed.

5. Give pedestrians the right of way. Avoid sidewalks.

6. Look out for cars pulling into traffic. Keep a sharp lookout for automobile doors that open suddenly.

7. Never hitch onto other vehicles. Never do stunts or race in traffic.

8. Never carry other riders—carry no packages that obstruct vision or prevent proper control of the cycle.

9. Be sure that your brakes are operating efficiently and keep your bicycle in perfect running condition.

10. Slow down at all intersections and look to the right and to the left before crossing.

11. Always use hand signals for turning and stopping. For a left turn, the left arm should be straight out; for a right turn the left arm should be extended, bent at the elbow with hand pointing upward.

12. Ride in a straight line. Do not weave in and out of traffic or move from side to side.

13. Avoid ruts, grooves or car tracks; if you must cross them, turn your wheels at right angles. Wet pavements may be slippery and gravel treacherous.

14. Avoid riding over curbs or other obstructions that might rupture your tires.

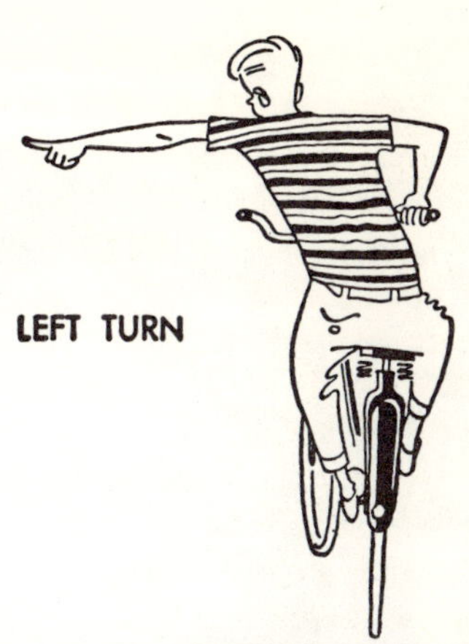

DON'T RIDE FRIENDS ON HANDLEBARS OR CROSSBARS

BE SURE YOUR HEAD AND TAIL LIGHTS ARE IN GOOD ORDER, YOUR BRAKE IN A-1 CONDITION

Here are some do's and dont's issued by the Bicycle Institute of America, Inc.

Test your skill at braking. You should be able to stop within a bike length.

BIKE SAFETY TESTS

Here are several useful safety tests; they are easy to set up. You will need a tape measure, chalk, white paint, 12 small boxes (2″ × 4″ × 4″), four stanchions or boxes about 18 inches high, and some score cards.

You may be able to obtain community support from a service club, the police department or the local auto club. These organizations will help organize and publicize the tests. In this way, more cyclists will be attracted to the event, and your community will become more safety conscious.

Here are the tests:

1. *Balancing at slow speed.* Mark a 3-foot-wide lane with white chalk and ask each rider to negotiate a 50-foot length at the slowest possible speed while staying within the lines.

2. *Steering.* Have contestants ride their bikes between parallel lines 4 inches apart without veering into the small boxes placed one foot apart on each side of the lines.

3. *Circle Riding*. Draw two circles, one inside the other. The larger should have a radius of 9 feet, the smaller a radius of 7 feet. To pass the circling test, the rider must negotiate the circles at normal speed, keeping within the two circles.

4. *Braking*. Here the cyclist must ride at a fair speed from one end of the testing area to the other until one of the judges suddenly commands him to stop. If he has good brakes and can control his wheel, he should be able to stop within a bike length.

5. *Maneuverability*. Place boxes or stanchions in a straight line, about 20 to 25 feet apart, on a 50-yard course. Each rider must negotiate the course at normal speed, weaving in and out of the boxes without touching them.

In "Circle Riding" the cyclists must keep within the lines while riding at normal speed. This test was photographed in Arlington, Virginia.

BIKE SAFETY QUIZ

Everyone should take an oral or a written test to evaluate his understanding of safety rules.

Here is a quiz you can give your friends or members of your bike club. State whether each sentence is true or false.

1. A cyclist riding in the street has the right of way over a pedestrian crossing the street or crosswalk. (F)

2. Two cyclists can ride side by side if they hold hands. (F)

3. If a rider is careful, he is safe in riding a bike that may be in bad condition. (F)

4. It is a good idea to walk your bike across heavy traffic. (T)

5. Since a bicycle is a vehicle, it should be ridden (in the United States) on the right-hand side of the street or highway. (T)

6. It is safe to pass a slow-moving car on the right side. (F)

7. If you ride your bicycle on the sidewalk, it is the responsibility of the pedestrian to keep out of your way. (F)

8. You signal for a left turn with your left arm and hand straight out. (T)

9. You signal for a right turn with your right arm held straight out. (F)

10. You should ride at least 3 feet away from parked cars. (T)

11. When crossing an intersection, a bicycle rider should look only straight ahead. (F)

12. It is safe to carry packages in both hands if you can ride without holding on to the handle bars. (F)

13. It is not safe to ride on icy or slippery streets. (T)

14. You don't have to stop for passengers getting off buses. (F)

15. In the schoolyard the cyclist has the right of way regardless of the number of students moving about and activities taking place. (F)

16. Only sissies observe all traffic regulations. (F)

17. After riding at any speed you should be able to stop within a bike length—if your brakes are good. (F)

18. Painting the rear fenders white increases the visibility of your bicycle at night. (T)

19. If you are careful, it is safe to take a passenger on your bike. (F)

20. Traffic signs for automobile drivers also apply to bicycle riders. (T)

Earning Money with Your Bike

After mastering cycling skills and safety rules, you may want to use your bike to earn money in your spare time. Odd delivery jobs exist in most communities. Now that you are a good rider, you are just the person to handle a delivery job.

Here are a few suggestions:

1. *Newspapers.* The newsboy's delivery job is the most popular among cyclists. Almost every town has a newspaper, daily or weekly, and the circulation department is always looking for dependable boys with bikes who can deliver papers to home subscribers. With a bike you can serve many more subscribers than if you were delivering on foot.

2. *Handbills.* Quite often small stores want someone to distribute announcements of sales in residential areas. On a bicycle you can cover lots of ground, putting handbills in mailboxes or under doors.

3. *Small packages.* Local retail stores and businesses may not have enough work for a regular commercial car delivery service, but they often employ a boy who has a bike. The druggist and grocer are good prospects. Printers, too, have a lot of small delivery work suitable for a cyclist. Contact these and other businessmen to find out if they can use your services. If you take on delivery work, you may need to buy a large wire basket which fits onto the handle bars.

Earning money may begin in a small way with only one store. But once you have made a successful record, you will always have the opportunity to take on more customers.

4. *Special delivery mail.* In smaller communities where there is no regular arrangement for handling special delivery mail, you may be able to get a job delivering such mail. Your local postmaster will be able to tell you whether any opportunities exist in your town.

5. *Telegrams.* You may be hired to rush telegrams to people. Bikes can get around easily through heavy traffic and operate effectively within a radius of a few miles. See your nearest telegraph office for a messenger's job.

6. *General delivery and errands.* Get word to the people on your block and in your neighborhood that you have a bike and are willing to run errands. You may be able to pick up a number of "accounts" this way. There are many persons who are too old or too sick to go to the store, and they would be glad to know of an errand or delivery service. Many mothers with small infants would probably also contact you for your services. You might even place a small ad in your local paper, saying that you are available and willing to run errands.

7. *Baby sitting.* A baby sitter who can furnish his or her own transportation is at a premium. If you can get to their homes and back again without involving your employers, you'll find yourself in great demand. Often a problem in baby sitting is that there is only one parent in a family, and he or she would have to leave the children alone while driving you home. If you have a bicycle, this difficulty disappears.

We have only scratched the surface. Once you have begun earning money with your bike, opportunities may unfold faster than you can handle them.

Care and Repair of Your Bike

Whether you are the owner of a custom-made racer or a standard balloon-tire model, your bike represents a considerable investment. It is probably your most treasured possession, perhaps also your means of earning spending money. Naturally, you will want to know how to care for your cycle in the best possible way.

After you and the members of your group or club have learned the fundamentals described on the following pages, you may want to introduce a bike repair course in your local trade or technical school. Such a course need not run longer than two or three weeks and can be included as part of a more extensive program on machine repair. Many bike clubs have had good luck sponsoring courses in bike repair.

FIXING A FLAT TIRE

If the flat was caused by a tack or nail, you'll have a fairly easy job fixing it; you will not have to take off the wheel. Just mark the tire and the rim at the point of puncture. If there is still some air in the tube, let it out by pressing the valve. You will now need a pair of pliers and a screw driver. Pry one side of the tire over the rim and pull out the part of the tube on which you marked the hole.

Use sandpaper or the scraper in a tire patch container to rough up

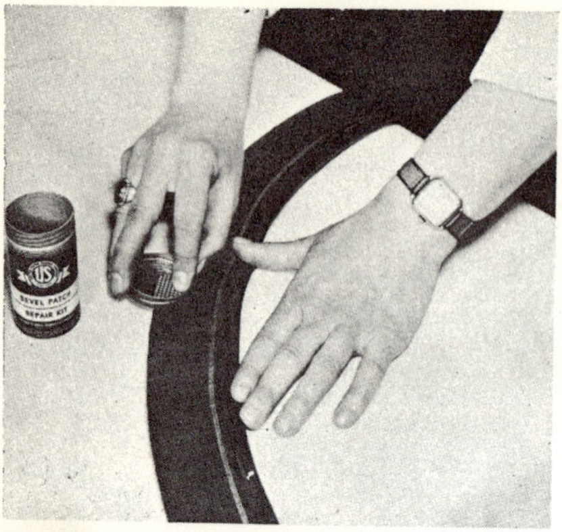

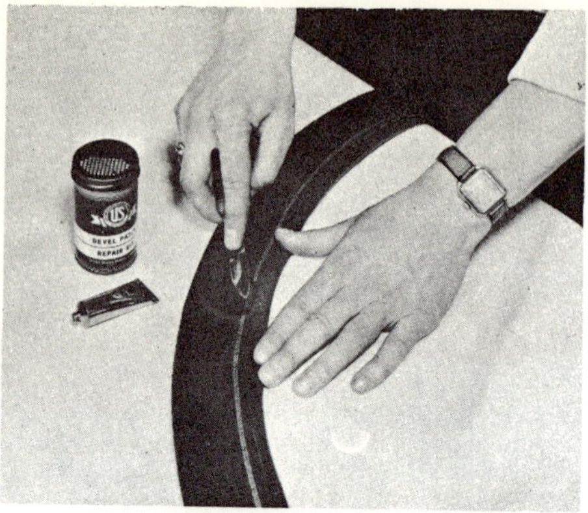

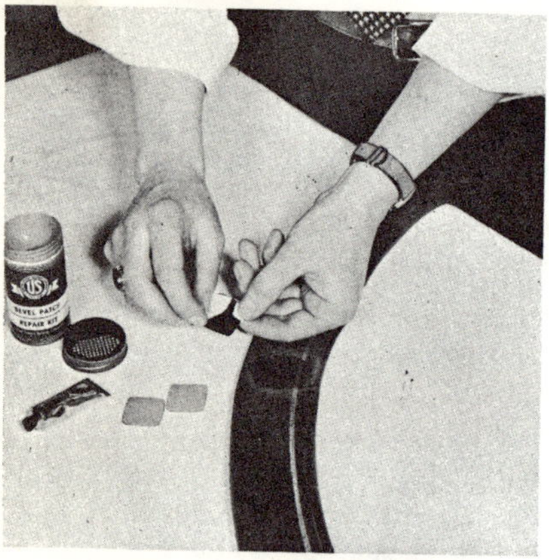

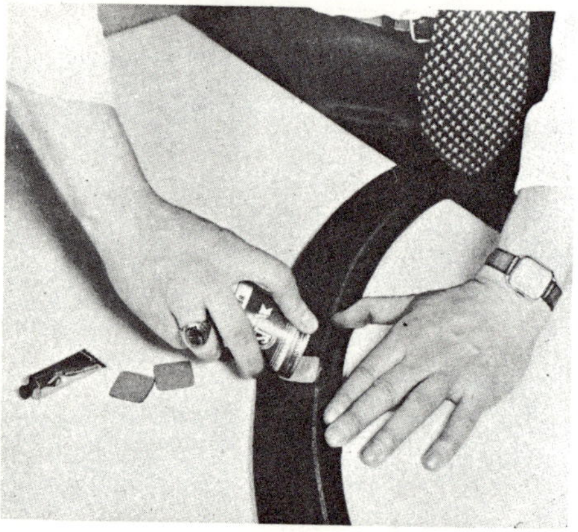

Steps in repairing a punctured tube: (Top left) Clean and roughen the surface around the puncture. (Top right) Then apply cement and spread evenly with the unsharpened side of a knife or similar object. (Center left) For the third step, remove backing from the patch. (Center right) Roll the patch to force out all the air bubbles. (Bottom) Wait 15 minutes for the cement to dry, place tube in the casing and mount the tire.

the tube surface. Unless you do this, the cement will not stick. Now, cement a patch over the damaged area.

If you can't find the hole on the tire, you will have to remove the wheel and take off the tire. It is best to begin by prying off the section of the tire opposite the valve, and work around until it is all removed. Inflate the tube and examine it closely for holes. It may be necessary to immerse the tube in water to locate the puncture. Any slight bubbling will indicate an air escape. Mark the hole and repair it as explained above. Your casing should then be cleaned of dirt, and any sharp particles which might have caused the damage should be removed.

CLEANING THE CHAIN

After considerable cycling, your chain will become gritty and clogged with small dirt particles. It is then time for a cleaning and lubricating job.

In order to do this, you will first have to remove the chain. Find the joint that binds the chain together. You will see a small spring connected to the joint. With a small screw driver you can force this spring, and your chain will come off.

Place the chain in a quart bottle half filled with kerosene and shake the bottle around until most of the dirt falls off the chain. Now take the clean chain out of the bottle and allow it to dry overnight in the open air.

After it is dry, place the chain in a pan. Pour heavy motor oil—about SAE 30—over the chain. Slosh the oil in and out of the links until you are sure the entire chain is covered with oil. You can use an old toothbrush to loosen stubborn dirt. After a few minutes take the chain out and wipe off the excess oil. Put the chain back on your bike and lubricate the links by rubbing them with a stick of graphite.

This special handling of your chain will provide smoother, quieter, and more efficient riding.

The chain should have no more than a one-inch slack when you move it up and down at its center. If your chain is too tight or too loose, you can adjust it by loosening the two nuts which hold the rear axle and either pulling in or pushing out the rear wheel, whichever is necessary to obtain the correct amount of tension.

HAVE YOUR BICYCLE CHECKED TWICE A YEAR BY A RELIABLE SERVICEMAN

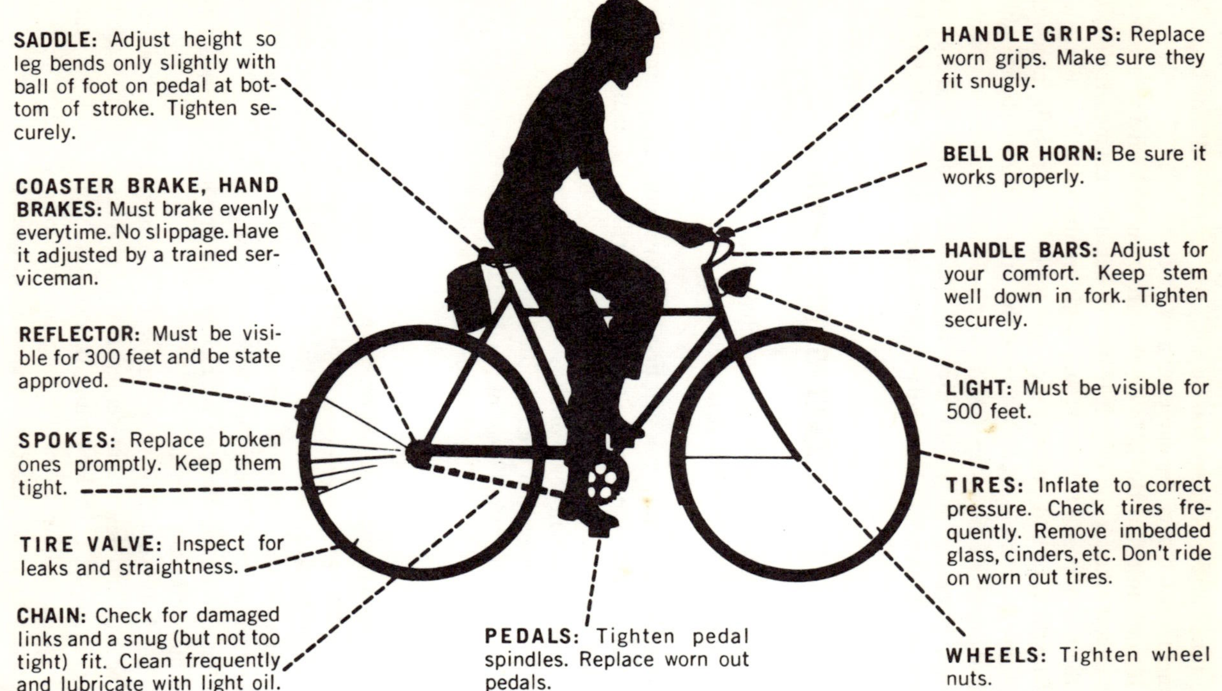

ALWAYS RIDE WITH CAUTION · TAKE GOOD CARE OF YOUR BICYCLE

GENERAL CLEANING AND OILING

You can easily wipe dirt off a bike with a soft rag, mild soap and warm water. Use nickel polish on your handle bars, tire rims and other nickel or chrome areas.

For periodic oiling use a thin oil. It will help if you first turn your cycle upside down. It is best to begin oiling at one end of your bike, carefully working toward the other end. Examine each movable part and oil it as you work along. At the front wheel, oil the movable parts of the rim brakes and the movable ends of the brake cables or rods. Usually at the front hub there is a small hole for oiling, but if your front wheel doesn't have a hole, place the oil at both ends of the hub.

Next, oil the handle bars and neck and the front fork bearings. The pedal bearings and pedal crank hanger should both be oiled frequently. At the back hub, oil should be placed in a small hole (similar to that in the front hub). If you have a variable gear, you should oil this part lightly too. Even the movable parts on accessories such as bells and horns should be oiled.

When it's time for the annual lubrication, you should also give your bike a complete overhauling. This can be done in spring, midsummer or just before putting your bike away for the winter. An overhaul includes cleaning, flushing with kerosene, and greasing the crank bearings, pedal bearings, front fork bearings, back and front wheel hubs and the chain. The first time you overhaul your bike, try to get someone who has done it before to work with you.

CLEANING THE CRANK HANGER, THE FORK AND THE FRONT WHEEL HUB

To clean your crank hanger, remove the pedal and the chain. With a strong wrench remove the hanger lock nut. As you take out each part, remember its position. Clean the shaft and other parts thoroughly with kerosene. Wipe them dry, and insert the crank back into the hub. Cover with light grease before you replace the other parts.

To overhaul the fork take out the handle bar stem. Turn off the head crown nut with your adjustable wrench. Remove the key washer and unscrew the cone. The fork will drop out of the head when it is raised.

Now, remove the bearings. Thoroughly flush the head of the fork with kerosene and wipe it dry. Remove all the grit in the ball bearings. Grease the bearings and reassemble.

To clean the front wheel hub first take off both nuts and washers. Pull the fork apart with your hands and slip out one end of the axle. Place one end of the axle on a bench and unscrew one side of the hub. The other cone and side of the axle can be removed together. Be sure the ball bearings do not fall out. All these parts should be washed in kerosene, then wiped dry. Before reassembling the hub, pack it with grease.

CLEANING THE REAR WHEEL AND PEDALS

To clean the rear wheel, first unscrew the hub nuts and washers. Take the fender arms off the axle. Undo the brake arm. Disconnect the chain by pushing the wheel in. Now, lift the wheel out of the frame. You can use an old toothbrush to clean fine particles of dirt out of the sprocket. If you have a coaster brake, do not use kerosene to clean the rear hub, as the kerosene will thin out the lubricant inside the hub.

To clean or replace your pedals, take off the nuts that hold the rubber treads. The treads and frame can now be taken off. Use care to see that you don't lose any of the ball bearings. Remove the lock nut and the key washer from the spindle. Wash all parts in kerosene, and then wipe them dry. The inside of the spindle should be packed with grease.

ADJUSTMENTS, HANDLE BARS, AND HANDLE GRIPS

After determining your saddle height, you will be able to adjust your handle bars for riding comfort. Look for the handle bar post bolt. Now loosen it with a wrench and tap it so the taper plug comes out. Stand over the front wheel of the bike and twist the handle bars to raise or lower them, according to the adjustment you want. Keep the handle bars very straight over the front wheel and tighten the post bolt. You can tilt your handle bars by loosening the clamp bolt, tilting the handle bar, and then tightening it.

If your handle grips fall off or are loose, you can tighten them with bicycle rim cement. First, clean and rough up your bar with sandpaper

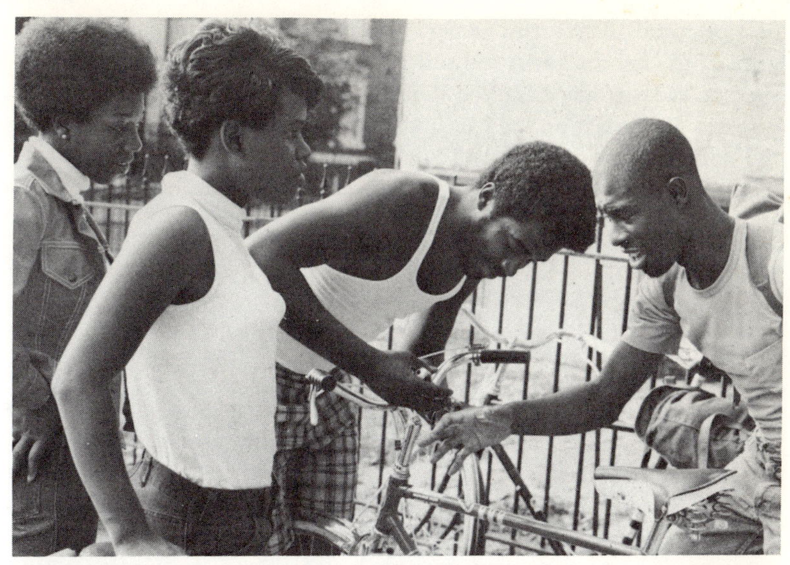

Straightening handlebars and repairing tires should be part of every competent cyclists' skill.
Photos Potomac area Council American Youth Hostel.

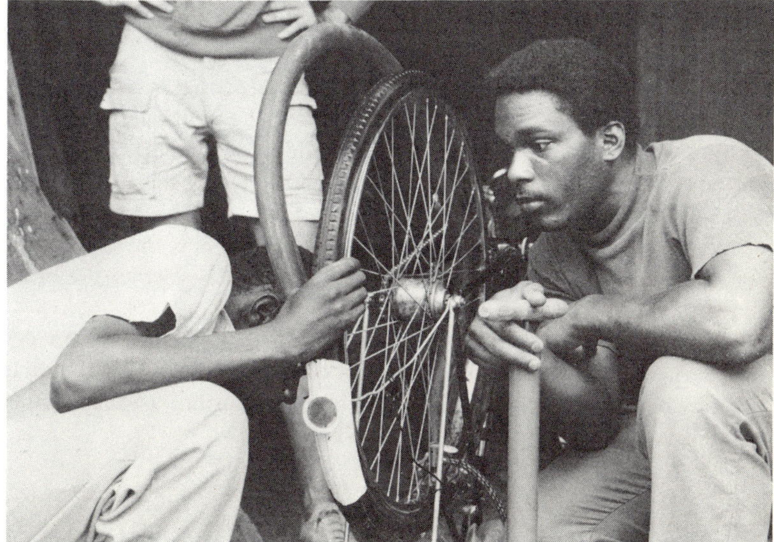

or steel wool. Apply rim cement to the bar and to the inside of the grip. If the handle bar is too short for the grip, put a wooden plug in the bar to lengthen it. If you don't, the grip will come off. Turn the grip as you push it on the bar, and of course, keep the finger ridges on the underneath side. Wipe off any cement that seeps under the edges of the grips. You can clean off excess cement with alcohol or naphtha.

TRUING THE WHEELS

In truing wheels your aim is to round out the rim. All you need are a spoke wrench and a nipple key. Turn your bike upside down so the wheels are free to turn as you test and work on them. Start with the spoke next to the valve so that you will be able to remember where you began. Now, test one spoke after another to see which are loose. When you come to a loose one, turn the spoke wrench on the nipple (the nut on the rim edge of the spoke). As you turn toward the left, you will see that the spoke becomes tighter.

If you find that the spokes are too long for the wheel, let the air out of the tires. Otherwise, the ends of the spokes may pierce the inner tube. Long spokes should be filed down at the ends.

You can pluck spokes as you would a musical string. When you hit a high note, you will know you have adjusted the spoke tight enough. Keep going until you have tightened all the loose spokes. Now, pluck all the spokes to see if all are of uniform sound, which means they have more or less the same degree of tension. Spin the wheel around and observe it carefully. Does it look round? Or does it seem to wobble? Apply your rim brakes if you have them to discover whether the brake pressure is even.

Uneven spoke tightness will make the wheel tend toward an egg shape. A wheel that is not round will wobble. Furthermore, if the cycle has rim brakes, the brake action will become uneven, as only certain parts of the rim will be reached by the brake.

When you store your bike for the winter, put it away upside down.

WINTERIZING YOUR BIKE

If you are going to put your bike away for the winter, first follow these steps:

1. Lubricate all movable parts and bearings.
2. Deflate tires.
3. Check spokes, tightening them or replacing broken ones.
4. Wipe spokes and all chrome parts with an oily cloth or vaseline.
5. Rub saddle soap into the seat. Work the soap in deeply, as this preserves the leather.
6. Store your bike by hanging it from the ceiling of your cellar, attic or garage. You can make hooks from half-inch iron rods attached to eye-hooks screwed into the ceiling. If you cannot hang your bike, turn it upside down so that it rests on its saddle and handle bars. Place paper or cloth over the wheels to protect them from dust.
7. Remember that winter storage should be in a cool place.
8. For a spring tune-up, repeat steps 1 and 3, inflate your tires to the proper pressure, check your saddle and handle bar adjustments as well as the operation of your lights and sounding device. Clean vaseline or excess oil off all chrome parts.

Bike Photography

Many aspects of cycling lend themselves well to dramatic pictures. Your friends, landscapes, villages, the people you meet on trips—all these furnish abundant photographic material.

But before you start shooting, you'd better review these basic principles of photography.

COMPOSITION

A well composed picture "hangs together." Your main concern should always be the subject. Ask yourself whether the composition leads the eye away from the subject or whether it dramatizes and emphasizes it. A good composition is a pleasing arrangement of background and subject matter. You have achieved it when all the objects in the picture appear to be balanced and harmoniously related to one another.

Like a moth, the human eye is attracted to light. We notice light-colored objects first, shadowy and darker objects later. Try to use lighting effects to create and strengthen your composition.

LIGHTING

A photograph is the result of light having been reflected from a selected object or group of objects which are recorded on film and later, on sensitized paper. If you want to take good snapshots, you must use light well. This means that you should obtain the right amount and the right quality of light. A picture should contain neither too many light

Camping trips provide dozens of opportunities for picture-taking and a photographic record of your outings will remind you of the good times you had.

masses nor too many dark masses—good composition results from an interesting arrangement of both.

You will have to experiment in order to become expert at using lighting effects. Try shooting from interesting angles or from various heights. Even if your first attempts aren't professional, you will enjoy experimenting with your camera.

POINT OF VIEW

What kinds of pictures do you want to create? You may want sharp, candid shots of your friends cycling or cooking around the campfire, or you may prefer more abstract shots involving unusual lighting effects—for example, a picture of a bicycle wheel with light hitting the spokes so as to create a delicate, sparkling effect. Silhouettes are interesting—perhaps a distance shot of cyclists moving across a plain. Reflections on water also make very unusual photographs.

As you can see, part of your photographic technique depends on your personal taste. This is what you bring to photography. Strive to master the principles of good picture taking—then, don't be afraid to be original. Experiment—try out your ideas. Your adventures with a bike will provide you with endless, fascinating material.

TAKING INTERESTING BIKE PICTURES

A camera is a helpful and useful accessory to any bike trip. With photos you can record and preserve your touring experiences. Years later snapshots will recall your memories of pleasant trips.

Dramatic shots can be taken through the spokes of a bike.

Even though you have to plan the pictures you take, they will be natural and interesting if the subjects are unposed.

Any bike photographer worth his salt will be able to dream up interesting picture ideas. But just to stimulate your creativity, here are a number of set-ups for cyclists.

1. *Shooting the subject through the bike spokes.* The spokes should be about 5 to 10 feet from your camera lens. Otherwise, your picture will be blurry. If you are shooting into soft light, you will get a silhouette.

Remember that the spokes and the subject beyond can only be photographed if your lens is "stopped down." That means there must be sufficient light.

2. *Portraits of cyclists on their bikes.* Shoot these from a low angle near the front wheel axle level. Be sure your subject's head is clear of the handle bars.

Whether you ride in New York's Central Park, as here, or down a winding country lane, your camera has a place in your equipment.

3. *Campfire pictures at night.* Take an atmospheric time-exposure using the fire as a light source. Be sure the light from the fire falls on the faces of your subjects.

4. *Bicycle in the foreground.* Shoot your bike at a distance of 10 to 20 feet, but pose it against a picturesque background about 20 to 40 feet distant. Stop down the diaphragm on this picture, or it may be out of focus.

5. *Using a road sign.* Watch for a sign such as, "Oberlin, 6 miles," or "Hostel" with an arrow pointing in the direction of the hostel. Try to catch some cyclists moving past the sign.

The sign should be about 4 to 10 feet away from the camera lens. Stop down the diaphragm if you want both the sign and the subject to be in focus. Remember, there must be full sunlight to "stop down."

6. *Cyclists silhouetted against the sky at dawn or dusk.* This is a particularly lovely shot if there is a lake in the background. Shoot into the light with the subject between the light and the camera. Be sure the light is soft; otherwise, your film will flare and you'll miss your shot. With soft lights you will need a wide aperture.

7. *Looking down a hill with cyclists moving on it.* Shoot this picture while the cyclists are in an interesting line or curve. Here, the value of the picture is in the design made by the riders.

8. *Shadows cast by riders and bike wheels.* Here, too, the beauty of the picture lies in the dramatic quality of the design.

9. *Details of significant parts of a bike.* You may want to have a picture of some part of the bike. Isolate an area of your cycle that would make an unusual "design" shot. Such a shot probably will be a closeup of handle bars, spokes, the sprocket or the lights.

10. *Candids shot as a record of your trip.* Take these "on the fly." Be ready for the casual, the funny, the unexpected. Your camera should always be loaded and ready for action. Pictures of activities should tell a story. Remember! Your subjects should look natural and unposed.

From the start of your trip to its triumphant end, your camera can capture every exciting moment. Picturesque bike trails are an ideal setting for those enjoyable hours shared with your friends and family.

11. *Framing your picture.* Find an archway, rock formation, group of trees or some similar structure to serve as a frame. Take pictures of cyclists riding toward you or away from you within the frame. If you use it artistically, such a frame will make your snapshot a genuine composition.

12. *A pictorial record or log of a trip.* Be sure to include all the major parts of the trip and some of the everyday happenings. Include shots of friends planning the trip, the departure, rest breaks, points of interest during the trip, campsites, overnight stops and the return.

Index